A LIFE WELL

Diaries of a FANY in the Special Operations Executive

* FANY = First Aid Nursing Yeomanry. founded in 1907 and now part of the Princess Royal's Volunteer Corps.

A LIFE WELL-LIVED

Diaries of a FANY* in the Special Operations
Executive

Fan Craig with
Malcolm Greenwood

BANKHOUSE

First published in the United Kingdom in 2014 by

Bank House Books

PO Box 3

New Romney

TN29 9WJ UK

www.bankhousebooks.com

British Library Cataloguing in Publication Data
A catalogue record for this book is available from the British Library

ISBN 9780957305878

Typesetting and origination by Bank House Books

Dedication

This book is dedicated to all the thousands of young women who have selflessly served as volunteers with FANY in war and peace from 1907 to 2010.

Contents

Acknowledgements

Above all I would like to thank Fan and all her family for honouring me with permission to tell her story.

I am grateful to Reuben Davison of Bank House Books for his patience and wise advice; to Claire Baldwin for her skill and patience in typing up my initial scribbled manuscript with remarkably few errors; to Jenny Holroyd for encouragement and advice; to Danny Ratcliffe for his beautiful artwork on the covers, produced despite the stress of renovating his first house and the discomfort of a broken rib; also to the many friends and neighbours who encouraged me to complete the task.

Special thanks to my wife Anne for her patience and encouragement, and for first introducing me to Fan.

Preface

When Fan agreed that I should tell her story for posterity, she exhorted me 'not to make it just another history book'. I explained that many of her readers were likely to be unfamiliar with the context of her story, both in peacetime and wartime. Accordingly I have sought to place her life within a historical setting, but this does not pretend to be another account of the Second World War, or events before and after. Therefore any errors or omissions are the author's own.

The story of Fan's experiences in the war during her service as a FANY volunteer seconded to SOE is recounted as she told it to me. As a signatory of the Official Secrets Act she will no doubt have kept to herself any matters that she feels come within the Act.

The reader will probably have read of the recent sad and lonely life and death of Eileen Nearne, another FANY volunteer at SOE who was one of those who survived service behind enemy lines in occupied Europe, where so many died at the hands of the Nazi regime after capture and torture.

Fan's story is one of similar dedication, but her good fortune in not being a field operative is the reason why she refused the offer of an award at the end of the war.

CHAPTER ONE

Early Days

'My mind to me a kingdom is ...
Look, what I lack my mind supplies.
Lo, thus I triumph like a king ...'
Edward Dyer

With the First World War only weeks old, 17 October 1914 was an inauspicious time to be born in Barnet. Vera Muriel Walters (Fan) was an afterthought to the family of a prosperous London printer; George Walters. Her mother Florence (née Palmer) was petite – only 4ft 10in – and very pretty. George was older. Fan's brother, also George, was thirteen years older than Fan, and her sister Lena was seven years older. George became a banker at Westminster Bank and to Fan was always a remote figure. Lena was a determined and attractive girl, whose dominant personality left Fan with a serious lack of self-esteem as a little girl.

The family home at the time of Fan's birth was 6 Warwick Terrace, Hadley, Hertfordshire, an Edwardian terraced house with a small garden. John Swain & Son, the business in which George Walters (senior) was an executive, was based in City Road, Holborn; George was employed at the branch in Barnet High Street. The company was best known as one of the originators of colour printing, for magazines such as *Vanity Fair*.

When she left school in 1915 Lena found an outlet for her extrovert personality as an assistant at a dress shop in Barnet High Street. She later married a journalist from the *Morning Post* and went to live in the suburbs south of the Thames. Fan was never close to her sister, who seems to have bullied her, perhaps unintentionally, but she did have an important if brief role later in Fan's life.

Fan's childhood seems to have been desperately lonely. Her father was a remote and distant figure who appears to have made little impression on her. He played virtually no part in her life. Fan's earliest memory is amazing. On 2 September 1916 a Zeppelin, Airship SL11, was shot down over Cuffley, Hertfordshire. This was the furthest north and west reached by Zeppelins, most of whose raids were on the East End and London's docks. Others that failed to reach London jettisoned their bombs over East Anglia in the attempt to reach home safely. The pilot in this, the first successful attempt by a fighter plane to bring down a Zeppelin, was William Leafe-Robinson, later awarded a VC for this exploit. The Zeppelin was at 1150ft, and the explosion when it was hit was visible all over North London and Hertfordshire. Fan remembers her father coming into her bedroom, picking her up and wrapping her in a rough brown rug. He took her to the other side of the house and stood with her in his arms at the window. She clearly remembers seeing the aircraft, and the Zeppelin exploding in a huge ball of fire. She can recall very little else of her infancy.

For some inexplicable reason Fan's father refrained from sending her to school when she reached the age of five, but a little later she attended Christ Church School for a few months, to which she could walk unaccompanied. This must have been an incredibly lonely time for her, since she rarely saw her father or her grown-up brother. Her mother is also a vague and indistinct figure, probably already sick with the illness that was to cause her death in 1922, when she was in her forties and Fan was only nine. At about the same time Fan fell ill with TB and was incarcerated for nine months in the isolation hospital at Brighton, where they had gone for a summer holiday. While she was there her mother's condition deteriorated and she died. No one told Fan until she came home from the sanatorium. She was never told what killed her mother but it seems possible that it was also TB.

Presumably in a moderately well-off middle-class household there was some domestic help, but Fan must have spent many lonely hours in her room until just after she developed TB. We gain an impression that her father was too busy to give much time to this unwanted late arrival, especially after his wife's death. He was preoccupied with business and his other interest, which was Barnet Football Club; he was chairman. When Fan was aged eight, however, George was persuaded by George junior that she should be sent to school, to avoid the School Board sending round the 'Board Man', a minor official whose role was to chase up truants and children who had never been sent to school. As an aspiring middle-class executive, George probably thought his tiny daughter was ill suited to the hurly-burly of a state school, so Fan was accordingly dispatched to an institution in Finchley, disparagingly nicknamed 'Big Sains' by its inmates and dismissed by Fan as a dame school. Officially, and rather pretentiously, it was called London College. Dame schools were those small private schools created by unmarried ladies in the nineteenth century to cater for the daughters of the middle classes, who were not expected to work for a living but to make a 'good' marriage. Fan was at this school from the age of nine to seventeen, in 1931, but she seems to have learnt little there, her education been entirely derived from Boots library in New Barnet. (In the years between the wars Boots the chemist also offered its customers a library service.)

Nothing much else survives in Fan's memory of her childhood; only snippets survive. She can recall reluctantly helping to make Christmas puddings. On one occasion an elderly neighbour found her wandering around the garden in her nightclothes, half asleep. She remembers the domestic help, a lady from across the road, making a play for her widowed father, who did not reciprocate her feelings. When she was ten (in 1924) her cousin, Ernest Walters, a stockbroker, who lived in Esher, visited to show off his new car – the first Fan had ever seen. This was the beginning of a life-long love of cars, which continues to this day. Fan does not appear to have seen Ernest again until 1941, by which time her life had taken some surprising turns. Her visit to Esher in 1941 coincided with an air raid, during which the french doors of Ernest's house were blown out by a bomb blast.

We are left with a poignant picture of a lonely small girl, physically and emotionally neglected by an elderly father, deprived of her mother at an early age, and consigned to a TB sanatorium for nine months with no visitors. She had little formal education or mental stimulation, although she recalls trips to the theatre, cinema and the seaside. She seems to have little recollection of friendships at any point in her childhood and adolescence, apart from a brief one in New Barnet. Aged seventeen, therefore, she left London College with nothing tangible to show for it: no friends, low self-esteem and afflicted by a dreadful shyness.

CHAPTER 2

Getting Started

'Let us then be up and doing,
With a heart for any fate;
Still achieving, still pursuing,
Learn to labour and to wait.'
Henry Longfellow

When Fan left school in 1931, the world was descending into a massive economic depression, and unemployment was heading towards the three million mark. Not that this mattered as far as George Walters was concerned. The printing business continued to thrive, and for many Londoners life continued much as before. This was the age of Art Deco, jazz, the boom in cinemas, high fashion and, above all from Fan's point of view, the liberation of women. Poverty was confined to the East End of London and the industrial areas of the North, Wales and Scotland. George Walters was the first in Hadley to have a phone and electricity: he was prospering, but constrained by his Victorian upbringing. His idea of a career for Fan was to make her his unpaid housekeeper. She had other ideas.

Without her father's approval, she signed on for a secretarial course at Pitman's College in Finchley, for which her brother paid.

For two years she learnt shorthand and typing, which at the time was the best route into a career for a middle-class girl.

At this point the first of many coincidences gave Fan an opportunity to accept a challenge. On a bus one day she fell into conversation with a neighbour whom she knew slightly, who said that she knew of a job opportunity. So it was that in 1933 Fan started her first junior secretarial job with a company in the City, Osbornes, which manufactured calendars, Christmas and greetings cards. Here she stayed for nine months, was very happy and did very well. Another chance meeting on the bus with the same neighbour led to Fan's second job, at Gillette Limited in City Road, where the neighbour worked. After a little while she was promoted to Gillette's offices on the Great West Road, fortuitously near her married sister Lena's home. Despite their mutual dislike, Fan found it convenient to spend several nights each week there rather than travelling to the distant northern suburb of Hadley. This gave her a chance of some social life.

CHAPTER 3
A Whirlwind Romance

'It was not in the Winter
Our loving lot was cast;
It was the time of roses –
We pluck'd them as we pass'd!'
Thomas Hood

By 1935 Vera Walters was twenty-one: petite, attractive and gradually overcoming the shyness and loneliness of her emotionally deprived childhood. Her social life was improving through the intervention of her brother, who took her to his tennis club in New Barnet. It was here that she was introduced to a young man who took an immediate interest in this pretty young woman.

Vera had acquired the family nickname Fan in childhood, from the phrase 'little Fanny Adams' – which referred to a precocious child. In view of later events this turned out to be an appropriate sobriquet. She retained it for the rest of her life, since she never really liked the name Vera. So from now on we had better think of her as Fan.

The young man who took a shine to her was Norman Aungiers, in Fan's words a 'handsome blond heart-throb'. Since she had no experience whatever of the ways of men beyond her aloof and distant, rather elderly father, and her almost equally distant much older brother, being courted assiduously must have been an exciting but confusing experience.

Norman Aungiers was the eldest of three brothers. His mother's brother owned a printing company, Edisons, in which he was employed, having trained at the Printers College. Norman owned a car (which at this time was quite unusual), giving him a distinct advantage in courtship. He was also brave enough to teach Fan to drive, again at this time an unusual accomplishment for a woman.

In 1937 Norman proposed marriage, and Fan accepted. Since she was marrying into a rival printing family, her father's response was to organise a lavish wedding. This must have been quite stressful since the families did not get on at all well, and the atmosphere on the day was clearly strained. The white wedding at Hadley parish church was held on 2 July 1938, with the reception at the Royal Hotel, Barnet. Fan refused to have Lena, whom she intensely disliked, as bridesmaid, choosing instead a friend from the Gillette office. Norman chose his brother John as best man. The happy couple took their honeymoon at Beer in Dorset, where it rained non-stop. They were very glad to get back to homemaking, and after they took a flat in Finchley a year of blissful happiness followed.

By this time the threat posed by Hitler's Nazi regime in Germany was becoming increasingly evident. As war clouds loomed, Norman, aged twenty-five and a member of the Honourable Artillery Company (a Territorial Army regiment based in the City), was duly commissioned a second lieutenant. In 1938 he was sent away to train with his regiment in 1938. The Munich Agreement and Chamberlain's famous 'peace in our time' meant that the HAC was recalled, and sent back to civilian life – but only briefly. The invasion of Czechoslovakia ensured that world war was unavoidable. The HAC returned to Somerset, therefore, for further training.

There, tragedy struck out of the blue. While crossing a field to post a letter to Fan, Second Lieutenant Aungiers fell victim not to Nazi gunfire but to an aneurism. Fortunately the clot in his brain killed him instantly, and there would have been no earlier symptoms. That Norman would not have known anything about it must have been of some comfort to Fan when news of his death reached her. She was staying with Norman's parents at the time, and must have been comforted by the presence of his mother, who had become very close to her.

Norman was given a funeral with full military honours, and was buried at Taunton. Fan was extremely distressed, and was unable to attend the funeral: Norman's CO took her out into the country in his car instead. Clearly the CO was very touched by these sad events, and he was to play an important role in the next chapter of Fan's life.

CHAPTER 4
Fan Goes to War

'When first I ended, then I first began;
Then more I travelled further from my rest
Where most I lost, there most of all I won.'
Michael Drayton

Norman's sudden death left Fan distraught with grief but determined to remain independent. Her memories of this sad time are buried. She moved in with Lena, in Putney, but by 1940 much pressure was being put on her by her sister's husband to move to a cottage in the country away from the bombs, with Lena's infant daughter Susan. Much as she disliked the idea, it was difficult to see an alternative, as a young widow with no home and with the Blitz raging.

Later in 1940 Fan felt that a change of job might help her to recover. She went to the Peter Jones Agency, looking for secretarial work, and was sent to a popular romantic novelist of the day, to type the manuscript of her latest work. This lady lived in Park Lane in some style, and when Fan arrived for her interview she was reclining on a sofa covered with a tiger skin rug.

After this job, Fan became secretary to the chairman of a coal merchant's business. He took pity on this sad but determined young widow and invited her to dinner. She took her sister with her, with whom she was still living. Fan discovered later that she had been set up to meet one of her employer's friends, a Major Douglas Packer, who was on a posting at the War Office.

By this time Lena had deserted her husband and baby, and as a result had been divorced. This brash, handsome, extrovert woman outshone the shy, sad and petite widow, and the major fell for Lena's wiles. He later married her. After the war they lived in Bangkok, where Douglas died. Lena returned to England and for a while lived with Fan, before remarrying and moving to Florida, where she had inherited a property on a golf course condominium, next door to General Patten's second in command.

Meanwhile Fan was still under pressure to be a childminder in the country, but at this opportune moment her late husband's CO contacted her, worried about how she was coping – and he took her to dinner at the Knightsbridge Grill. His view was that on no account should she submit to this well-meant bullying by the family, but should rather do what Norman would have done in the war, focusing Fan's anger and grief into action.

Norman's mother, Fan's closest friend among the extended family, died in 1946. Fan lost touch with the rest of the family for many years, but eventually visited Norman's father, and still hears from Norman's younger brother Jasper, who as a lieutenant in the Navy served on the Murmansk convoys during the war. He now lives in South Africa.

Fan was waiting to be called up for national service, aged twenty-seven and with no family ties (becoming a family drudge would probably have exempted her from this). Many women of her class chose to serve in the Women's Land Army, working on farms, while others of all classes were directed into factory work, manufacturing munitions. Neither option appealed to Fan. The alternatives were the women's military services, the WRENs, WRAFs, WRAACs or ATS, and she was prepared to consider any of these. So it was that Fan set out with her friend Winifred Hey (sister of a friend of Norman's) to check out the possibilities. This, remember, was during the Blitz, when the Luftwaffe was making a determined effort to bomb London into submission, quite possibly as a prelude to invasion, while the Spitfire and Hurricane pilots of the RAF fought the Battle of Britain over London and the south-east. Submarine warfare was threatening to starve the country of food and war supplies. Britain seemed to be standing alone against impossible odds. It was in this atmosphere of fear that Fan set off with her friend to check out the women's services. Sad to relate, they were deeply unimpressed by them all. Fan finds it difficult to explain why: perhaps she is guilty at feeling these services were too proletarian for two sparky young middle-class girls. Whatever the reason, they decided to pop into Harrod's for a cup of tea and to rethink their plans. Here, Winifred suggested over a cup of tea at Harrods that they should visit another outfit: the First Aid Nursing Yeomanry (later Women's Transport Service & Princess Royal's Volunteer Corps). The die was cast.

The origin of the FANYs can be traced back to Kitchener's expedition to the Sudan in the late 1890s. A Captain E.C. Baker, serving as a cavalry sergeant major, was wounded in action, an experience that prompted him to have the idea of forming of a detachment of females, on horseback (they were required to provide their own horse!), to provide mobile first aid assistance between frontline units and field hospitals. The FANY (PRVC) was duly formed in 1907. Its purpose then (as now) was to assist the Military and Civil authorities. Initially it was to put into practice Barker's original idea- to be a first aid link between frontline fighting units and field hospitals. On the outbreak of the First World War in August 1914 the FANY offered their services to the British Military Authorities, but this offer was rejected. The same offer was made to the hard-pressed French and Belgium armies, and this time was accepted.

It should be remembered that the FANY is a purely voluntary organisation, a registered charity now as then, and is the only female voluntary yeomanry. The concept of a voluntary yeomanry goes back to the Napoleonic Wars, when many units were formed to counter any attempted French invasion. The FANY is affiliated to the TA but is not part of it.

In September 1914 the first elements turned up in Antwerp for service. They acquitted themselves with great courage in what was a volatile period of open warfare. They drove ambulances, established troop canteens and soup kitchens, and ran field hospitals. When

Belgium was completely overrun and the war settled into a stalemate on the Western Front, a line of trenches and fortifications stretching from the coast of Belgium south-east to the Swiss border, the FANY were accepted by the British authorities, for whom they provided the same services throughout the war. Many members were rewarded for their bravery and devotion, with awards and medals, by Belgium and France as well as the UK government.

The composition of the FANY from its inception to the start of the Second World War was almost exclusively upper-middle-class. The young women who joined were adventurous and independent, eager to break away from the stereotypical role of homemaker and hostess. As they had little formal education, a good marriage was the only career choice available. These girls were not prepared to be a decorative chattel of a rich man, though; they wanted adventure. They had to be pretty well to do, however. This was a voluntary organisation, so girls who were accepted had to buy their own uniform and equipment, and have a sufficient allowance to keep them. They also had to be able to ride, and have no domestic ties. This was still the case in 1940.

Women of lower social class were likewise drawn into service in both wars in public, commercial and industrial work, taking the place of men who were fighting. They did everything from driving trams to working on the land or in munitions factories. Women too old to serve in the forces or the factories, but with a spouse in a reserved occupation, did their bit in voluntary services, for example the Women's Voluntary Service (WVS). This was true of both wars, but already by 1916, it had become necessary to form women's auxiliary services of various kinds. By 1940 it had become necessary to conscript young women with no domestic ties to either uniformed paramilitary organisations (the ATS, WRENs, WAAF) or into war work. The experience of service was to transform the role of women in society, emancipating them from their subservient status and establishing the roots of feminism.

At the end of the First World War it was thought to be unlikely that total war could happen again, and voluntary organisations formed for war service were mostly disbanded. The FANY, however, had none of this, and it was decided to maintain a rump organisation in case of a national crisis. At the outbreak of the

Second World War the FANY volunteered its services. Its role began to change. The FANY supplied the initial motor driver companies of the ATS, without losing their identity as FANYs. Other recruits, according to their skill and background, were transferred to the newly formed Special Operations Executive (SOE). This is where Vera Aungiers was to serve from 1941 to 1945 with great distinction.

Since 1945 the FANY has continued in existence, now specialising in communications for the Army and the City of London Police. Members are now as throughout its history, volunteers resident in or near London. They are trained in radio communications, paramedical skills, map reading, advanced driving, and casualty bureau documentation. In 1999 the FANY was officially renamed the Princess Royal's Volunteer Corps, but is still referred to as FANY (PRVC); the FANYs.

In the course of this account of Fan's life we will meet many of her colleagues who served with distinction on secondment to the SOE.

CHAPTER 5

A Just War

'Now all the youth of England are on fire,
And silken dalliance in the wardrobe lies ...'
William Shakespeare

As England, along with much of the developed world, struggled in the economic aftermath of war, with the boom and then collapse of world markets, the great crash of stock markets in 1929 and the subsequent Great Depression, thoughts of war recurring were repressed. Even in the 1930s, as Hitler seized power in Germany and began to test his neighbours' resolve, appeasement was the buzzword.

It was thought by most observers that no nation was ever likely to allow a repeat of the horrors of trench warfare. Disarmament conferences came and went, their provisions meticulously observed by Britain but evaded by Hitler. Reinforcing this attitude was the belief among the educated classes in Britain that Hitler's regime was a powerful model for the regeneration of a nation ravaged by economic disaster. Roads were built, jobs created by surreptitious rearmament, young people disciplined and corrupt politicians ousted. The 1936 Berlin Olympics seemed to mark the peak of Germany's renaissance. There was even a good deal of sympathy for

Hitler's blatant anti-Semitism. Henry Williamson, author of *Tarka the Otter* and a hero of the First World War, was typical of this cast of mind: 'Here at last is someone [Hitler] who has perceived the root causes of war in the unfulfilled human ego and is striving to create a new human-fulfilled world.'

These attitudes permeated the world view of a generation of British politicians, who instinctively felt that the way forward was to placate the needs of Germany. The reoccupation of the Rhineland in 1936 (it had been ceded to France at the Treaty of Versailles in 1919) and the occupation of Austria in 1938 were thus deemed to be an acceptable price for cooperation with Germany, appeasement making a war of revenge much less likely. Even the invasion of Czechoslovakia in 1939, to 'liberate' the mainly German population of the province of Sudetenland, was accepted. Munich, and Chamberlain's 'piece of paper', was the desperate last chance to save the peace. In the eyes of more pragmatic figures it provided a breathing space during which we could rearm.

In reality the reoccupation of the Rhineland was the last chance to call Hitler's bluff. If the old allies had resisted firmly, Hitler might have been stopped in his tracks. After that, he could see no danger of any nation thwarting his ambitions. Within the year he had invaded Poland, and there was no alternative left to a broken prime minister. On 3 September Chamberlain told the nation that there was no alternative but to declare a state of war between Britain and Germany.

The French were relying on the Maginot Line to ensure no repeat invasion. This immense line of fortifications stretched the length of the Franco-German border, and appeared to generals, who were still thinking in terms of the First World War, to be completely impregnable. Unfortunately the Franco-Belgium border was completely undefended against the German Wehrmacht, which was established there by autumn 1939.

A British Expeditionary Force was dispatched to France in September 1939, although pitifully inadequate in the face of massive German forces. A period of 'phoney war' ensued, during which nothing happened on the continent. Germany's intentions were made clear on the first day of war, though, when the liner *Athenia*, carrying 200 children to safety in America was torpedoed and sunk in the Atlantic. Soon afterwards (19 September) HMS *Courageous* was sunk by a U-boat, as were several merchant ships. On 16 October the battleship HMS *Royal Oak* was sunk, ominous signs of the vulnerability of both the Royal Navy and the merchant fleet.

Germany's 1939 peace pact with Russia's Stalin ensured that there would be no 'second front' to divide Nazi forces. On 10 May 1940 the Wehrmacht attacked the Albert canal north of Liège, and the defeat and occupation of Belgium, Holland and North France rapidly followed. By 27 May the advance had pushed on almost to the Channel coast at Dunkirk, to which the vastly outgunned BEF had retreated in disarray. The Royal Navy, assisted by an assortment of ferries and merchantmen, and a flotilla of small craft (30–100ft) commandeered under Operation Dynamo, successfully evacuated 338,000 exhausted troops, most of whose equipment had been destroyed or abandoned.

At home it was clear that it would not be possible to feel detached from the action in Europe. In 1939 the evacuation of children from vulnerable cities to the countryside began. The threat of air attack was very real, and a blackout was imposed everywhere after dark. No lights of any kind were to be shown, as they might guide incoming bombers. The ringing of church bells was prohibited: they were only to be used to warn that an invasion had begun. Fuel and food were soon in short supply, and food rationing began on 8 January 1940. Allies were required to register, and those with German connections were later interviewed. Young men aged twenty to twenty-two were called to the colours. Factories were turned over to production of war materials. Men too old to serve were conscripted to retrain in engineering or mining.

The mood among the people in 1939–40 was of boredom combined with fear and trepidation. But Dunkirk triggered a change of mood, fired by the memorable speeches of Winston Churchill, who evoked 'the Dunkirk spirit' of heroism against the odds and a fierce pride in the fact that Britain stood alone against the real threat of invasion. With hindsight, however, it cannot be said whether Hitler ever seriously intended to do so. On 17 June France sought an armistice.

It is in this context that we must place the genesis of the SOE, its relationship with the FANYs and the beginning of Fan's war.

CHAPTER 6
England Stands Alone

'No coward soul is mine,
No trembler in the world's storm-troubled
sphere ...' *Emily Brontë*

I t was in this atmosphere, compounded of fear and anger, doubt and determination, uncertainty and defiance, that Fan Aungiers took the fateful steps that took her into a great adventure. She was to experience every emotion from hilarious misadventure to heart-rending sadness.

The events that were to bring Fan into the secret war of the SOE began in 1940. Although Britain was ill equipped in 1939 to fight a world war, behind the scenes preparations had begun, with steps being taken to create two departments that were the predecessors of SOE. GS (R) (research into irregular warfare) stemmed from the War Office, and dealt with activities to be carried out by uniformed soldiers. By 1939, redesignated MI (R), its first director was Royal Engineer Major (later Major-General) J.C.F. Holland, who was assisted by Major Colin Gubbins. The second group, Section D, was formed by the SIS; its commander was Major Lawrence Grand, also of the Royal Engineers. Its function was undercover warfare against an invading force.

By spring 1940 the real fear of invasion led to the formation of a further force, Auxiliary Units. These stemmed largely out of recruits from the Local Defence Volunteers (later the Home Guard), which had been established for over-age men, those too young to serve and those in reserved occupations, such as farmworkers. The Home Guard has been immortalised in the TV series *Dad's Army*, which gently caricatured the organisation's incompetence and innocent courage.

The Auxiliary Units were highly secret, and their existence was not revealed until the 1950s. Recruits came through the recommendations of local people, and included landowners, farmers, gamekeepers and others who knew an area's terrain. Recruits were enrolled in the Home Guard and wore its uniform, but were not involved in its normal military training. Each tiny unit was provided with a hidden underground hide, known as its operational base, equipped for sleeping and cooking, with stores of food and water. Radio communications equipment, weapons, ammunition and explosives were provided. Members signed the Official Secrets Act and were sworn to secrecy. This vow was taken very seriously, which is how their existence remained hidden for so long. It is remarkable but true that in about 2002 a very elderly farm worker in East Anglia turned up at an army depot asking for advice. He was the last survivor of his Auxiliary Unit, and felt that he should tell the Army where their operational base was, so that the wartime stores could be removed. Ever since the war he had kept the weapons clean and in full working order, alongside stacks of highly volatile explosives and ammunition.

The Auxiliary Units were set up by Colin Gubbins, now promoted to colonel. Field Marshal Ironside, to whom Gubbins had been aide-de-camp in 1919 and was now C-in-C Home Forces, agreed to provide the supplies needed. Gubbins's experience on the military mission to Poland in 1939, and as Commander of the Independent Companies (forerunners of the Commandos) during the Norway Campaign in 1940, for which he was awarded the DSO, fitted him entirely for this role, and also for his later position as director of the SOE. Gubbins worked in great secrecy, reporting only to Ironside and to Winston Churchill (now the prime minister) weekly. Within weeks the organisation was in place, with 5,000 men (and a few women) recruited. Their strength was concentrated up to 30 miles inland, from South Wales to Scotland round the south and east coasts, where a seaborne invasion was anticipated.

A research laboratory at Stevenage, operated by Section D, produced a new form of plastic explosive ideal for use by the Auxiliary Units, and it was this that first brought Gubbins in touch with the FANYs. Phyllis Bingham, who had joined the FANY, and was later to become its commander, was a family friend of Gubbins, and he contacted her in the hope that the FANYs could package the explosive safely – and this they did, using small tie boxes. The organisation also provided drivers for the Auxiliary Units.

By May 1940 it had been decided that section D and MI(R) could not be merged, and that a fresh start was required now that almost the whole of North-West Europe was occupied by the Germans. The invasion of Britain still seemed to be a possibility, which meant it was necessary to plan underground response with clandestine units. On 27 May 1940 the Chiefs of Staff recommended to the War Cabinet that a special organisation should be put in place as a matter of urgency. A War Cabinet minute of 19 July approved the creation of a Special Operations Executive, to coordinate 'sabotage, subversion and secret propaganda against the enemy overseas', under the Minister of Economic Warfare, Hugh Dalton. This appears an unlikely choice, as he was a left-wing economist. Churchill's exhortation to him was to 'set Europe ablaze'. Sir Frank Nelson, a former MP and diplomat, was to head SOE, with banker Charles Hambro as his deputy. Nelson's code title of CD was passed to his successors. Gubbins, having established the Auxiliary Units, was ready for a new challenge, and Dalton appointed him Director of Training on 18 November 1940.

In his new role Gubbins rapidly established a network of stations, training establishments where potential agents from many nations would learn their skills, and holding houses for agents who were about to be sent into the field. There were eventually seventy-seven training stations, and the existence and purpose of any unit could not be divulged.

This done, Gubbins was instructed to undertake the planning of operations. Initially SOE was based in two apartments at Berkeley

Court, near Baker Street station, but this soon became inadequate, and the head office of Marks and Spencer at 64 Baker Street was requisitioned as the administration base and communications centre. It was here that Fan Aungiers was to first meet Gubbins; and embark on her part in the secret war.

The experience gained by the FANY driving ambulances and other vehicles in France and Belgium during the First World War meant that a change of title and role was considered between the wars. The organisation was to be renamed Women's Transport Services (FANY), but this name never stuck. When the Auxiliary Territorial Service (ATS), a women's corps, was founded in 1938, it was decided that the FANY should become part of it, although retaining a separate identity. In 1939 this promise was revoked, however, and the FANY drivers were absorbed into the ATS, supplying ten motor companies of 150 girls each. FANY was to cease to be independent, and FANY HQ staff were to lose their ATS pay. FANY had always been fiercely independent, though, and Marion Gamwell and her sister Rose, veterans of France in the First World War, returned from Northern Rhodesia to form the 'free' FANY. Recruitment continued under Marion, the redoubtable commandant, who insisted on surnames only with no mention of rank. It was this formidable lady who recruited Fan.

Gamwell's approach made FANY ideal from the SOE's point of view. Her FANY recruits suffered from none of the restrictions that rendered other women's units unsuitable. They could be sent anywhere, were not prevented from carrying and using arms, and there were no practical difficulties – such as the requirement for there to be so many bathrooms for a given number of servicewomen. Phyllis Bingham, originally Gamwell's secretary, became indispensable from 1940 to 1944 as officer in charge of recruitment of FANY for service with SOE. She expected the girls to turn their hands to any job, and to do as they are told.

The high sense of duty of the FANYs made them indispensable to SOE in administrative, teaching, driving and domestic roles. Their postings could not be revealed even to next of kin, especially those whose work was in wireless communications, coding and so on. Extreme secrecy was maintained and, as for the rest of SOE, next of kin had no idea where their relations were or what they were engaged upon. This was why it was important to recruit women without family ties if possible.

FANYs often never left the perimeter of the training stations for many months, whether in Britain or overseas. Some, whose duties were domestic, found themselves doing boring and repetitive work with little chance of promotion. The men under training needed compassionate but firm treatment, and romantic liaisons were forbidden.

Some FANYs, often those with dual nationality, served with distinction in the field. Others, including Fan, were involved at SOE HQ at 64 Baker Street, rendered anonymous by the sign at the entrance, ISRB (Inter Services Research Bureau), which provided a plausible reason for the comings and goings of many men and women of different nationalities and uniforms. At Baker Street, as it was known throughout SOE, some FANYs were recruited (like Fan) because of their education at London secretarial colleges. All FANY volunteers were classed as ensign, officer status, but in terms of the Regular Army were non-commissioned other ranks. Of these a few were promoted, like Fan, first to corporal. Later, when Fan was promoted to captain, having reached a senior staff posting as aide-de-camp (ADC) to Colonel Douglas Dodds-Parker, she had in Army terms reached the equivalent of major.

Everyone, of whatever status, had to undertake basic training, and remained volunteers. Others undertook weapons and parachute training or radio communications training before being dispatched into field activities in Europe. A very small number of these, with staff jobs, became indispensable to senior officers, and were sent to North Africa and Egypt. Fan was to be one such.

CHAPTER 7

A Friend for Life

'But if the while I think on thee, dear friend,
All losses are restored and sorrows end.'
William Shakespeare

As we have seen, the driving force behind the establishment of SOE was Colin Gubbins, and his authority rested heavily on Churchill's willingness to consider any initiative, however unusual. Without the prime minister's approval the doubts, prejudices and self interest of others might well have strangled SOE at birth: the Foreign Office, MI5, MI6, the War Office and the regular armed services were strongly opposed to its formation. Labyrinthine disputes continued for several years, but are not directly relevant to our story. The Establishment attitude to SOE is neatly illustrated in a letter dated 1 February 1941 from Air Chief Marshal Charles Portal to George Jebb: 'I think the dropping of men dressed in civilian clothes for the purpose of attempting to kill members of the opposing forces is not an operation with which the Royal Air Force should be associated. I think you will agree that there is a vast difference in ethics between the time honoured operation of dropping a spy from the air and this entirely new scheme for dropping what one can only call assassins!'

In other words, it isn't really cricket, chaps! It is easy to see how horrified the Establishment would have been by the use of female agents. Portal's attitude goes some way to explaining why SOE was plagued throughout the war by the unwillingness of the RAF to supply sufficient air transport to deliver, support and retrieve agents.

In July 1941 Hugh Dalton wrote to Lord Halifax, the foreign secretary:

> we have got to organise movements in enemy occupied territory comparable to the Sinn Fein movement in Ireland … This must use many different methods, including industrial and military espionage, labour agitation and strikes, continuous propaganda, terrorist acts against traitors and German leaders, boycotts and riots.
>
> What is needed is a new organisation to coordinate and assist the nationals of oppressed countries who must themselves be the direct participants. We need absolute secrecy, a certain fanatical enthusiasm, willingness to work with people of different nationalities, complete political reliability … But the organisation should in my view be entirely independent of the war office machine.

All this was completely alien to the mindset of officers in the regular services. This partly explains why the apparently haphazard recruiting process worked as well as it did. The appointment of Colin Gubbins was a master-stroke. M.R.D. Foot points out that 'SOE was like a club, for membership was by invitation only.' It was impossible to apply or put oneself forward; potential members were carefully scrutinised, and penetration by the enemy was rare. A vast array of talents was required in both staff and field operatives, not just bravery, but methodical organisation, fluency in languages, technical skills, explosives skills, secretarial skills and ciphering skills.

In view of the role of women in society at the time it is not surprising that the women's services were not expected to be trained for or undertake frontline duties. Driving and paramedical skills, administrative skills and even flying skills could be employed. For example, a unit of women pilots was employed to deliver anything from Spitfires to transport aircraft. It is all the more surprising, therefore, that SOE employed women as agents deep in enemy territory, prepared to kill and at great risk of death. The recruitment of women to SOE from the other women's services, and direct from civilian life, was down to Captain Selwyn Jepson being appointed as SOE's senior recruiting officer. In an interview by the Imperial War Museum after the war, Jepson made the following comment:

> I was responsible for recruiting women for the work, in the face of a good deal of opposition from the powers that be. In my view women were very much better than men for the work. Women, as you must know, have a far greater capacity for lonely courage than men. Men usually want a mate with them. Men don't work alone, their lives tend to be always in the company of other men. There was opposition from most quarters until it went up to Churchill, whom I had met before the war. He growled at me, 'What are you doing?' I told him and he said, 'I see you are using women to do this', and I said, 'Yes, don't you think it is a very sensible thing to do?' and he said, 'Yes, good luck to you.' That was my authority!

What remarkably perceptive comments!

Agents of both sexes possessed qualities rare in conventional officers. Despite their unconventional duties and dress code, SOE people were given a rank and number in one of the three regular services (usually the Army) if they did not already possess one, and were on the General List (of officers). Most staff officers were given the rank of lieutenant or captain (Army) or equivalent.

It is wrong to suppose that SOE personnel received lavish pay or other material reward for their extraordinary service: they were paid according to their rank. In fact FANYs seconded to SOE, at whatever rank and whether serving on staff or field posts, were volunteers, pure and simple, and received no pay, only subsistence, and were even required to buy their own uniforms before being accepted as a FANY! This was true of even Vera Atkins, a GSOIII (captain) who was regarded by a head of training section as 'really the most powerful personality in SOE'.

Since Colin Gubbins was to have such an influence on Fan's life during and after the war, we should perhaps say something more about the man and his career. Major-General Colin McVean Gubbins SOE code CD was a Highland Scot, of slight build and full of restless energy. He served during the First World War in the Royal Artillery, ending the war with DSO, MC, MID, 1914 Star, and British War and Victory Medals. He remained in the Army after the Armistice, fighting in Russia in 1919 with the White Russians (against the new Communist regime), and in 1920–1 fought a losing struggle in Ireland. He left the Army at that point and became an executive for Ford in Paris, his fluency in French, German and Russian being an advantage.

Gubbins was recalled to service in 1939 in the rank of major, being appointed chief of staff of the British Military Mission to Poland in summer 1939, later receiving the Croix de Vaillance. In 1940 (now a brigadier) he commanded the first commando operation in Norway, before being appointed Director of Operations and Training at SOE in May 1940, as we have seen. In 1944 he produced the Foxley Report, which recommended the assassination of Hitler, a suggestion that had a mixed reception: the regular services took the view that Hitler was a totally incompetent commander in chief, and therefore Britain's best ally. It was thought that his replacement by a competent officer, with Hitler perceived as a martyr, would make the final stages of the war much more difficult. By this time Gubbins was a major-general and Executive Head of SOE. After the war he was awarded the Legion d'Honneur, and was appointed KCMG.

Clearly a fine soldier and staff officer, a brilliant lateral thinker and a very brave man, it is as an inspirational leader, and staunch friend that Gubbins is remembered by those who knew him, including Fan. In 1941, in the darkest hours of the war, their paths were to cross for the first time.

CHAPTER 8

Fan Gets Lucky

'And here I am, enjoying it all
On this pandemonium day.'
Win Wilcock

We left Fan and her friend Winifred in Harrod's, having a cup of tea and deciding what to do next – and agreeing on the spur of the moment to seek an interview with the FANYs. By chance, Harrod's is near the vicarage of St Paul's Church, on Wilton Place, Knightsbridge, which had been taken over as the FANY recruitment centre. It was known as Bingham's, as Phyllis Bingham was chief recruiting officer.

Fan is unsure who interviewed her; she thinks it was Marion Gamwell herself. She was completely overawed at first, and describes her interviewer as a 'dragon'. Since she had no title and no horse, she felt far too lower-middle-class for the outfit. Since the two girls knew little of the FANYs' history and role, they did not know they possessed vital skills. Nearly seventy years later, Fan cannot understand how she came to qualify, except that as a young war widow with no children she had no ties. Unlike other recruits to FANY, her financial means were limited. Her limited formal education meant that she had no foreign language skills. She had, however, learnt to drive, and was no longer the shy and lonely girl of ten years earlier. She had a set of very useful practical office skills, including shorthand and typing. The feisty, determined and resourceful officer she was to become must have been evident to Bingham, and later to Colin Gubbins.

Gamwell decided to accept both the girls – but there was a major snag. She pointed out that the FANYs were volunteers: there was no pay. This they could cope with, but then they were told that they had go to Lilywhites to buy a complete uniform, before being sent for their final selection tests. The uniforms cost £300 each! The girls felt this was a bridge too far, since they might not pass the selection tests – and £300 was a year's wages in civilian life. Fan's feisty nature overcame her shyness, and she insisted (tactfully, she claims!) that they were only prepared to proceed if they could go to the selection board in an 'ordinary tweed suit'. Bingham must have met her match, because she capitulated. Fan guesses she was desperate for drivers.

In that dark and severe winter they found their way to Lady Boileau's country house in Norfolk, the only FANY training centre, where they were put through an intensive course in first aid and vehicle maintenance. Then came the tests. At this early stage it was still assumed that the FANYs would be ambulance drivers – but since Dunkirk the previous year front-line ambulances had become less critical, and a wide range of driving duties was envisaged within the ATS. The selection tests had not changed, however. Each recruit was required to strip down and reassemble an ambulance engine, drive off, and follow a route without road signs (removed for the duration) in limited time. The second test was a role play, in which the recruit was told that the house was a field hospital, and that her task (with Gamwell sitting alongside) was to recover a badly wounded soldier from the far end of the long drive as rapidly as possible. The ambulance was then to be reversed around the rosebed in front of the palatial entrance, and up to the front door. This was no problem for Winifred, who was an elegant 5ft 8in tall as well as an experienced driver. Fan, on the other hand, had claimed to be 5ft 2in (the lower limit), but was in fact 5ft exactly. Disaster struck. The vehicle was probably a Ford or Bedford 1½ ton box van with narrow cab, large box body (with no wing mirrors and extending about 9in either side of the cab), large steering wheel and a crash gearbox requiring double de-clutching. Exhorted by the 'dragon' to 'hurry or this soldier is dead!', Fan found that reversing round a turning circle was a step too far. Leaning out of the cab to see where she was going she lost control, stalling with a jerk and throwing herself out into a neglected rosebed. The dragon stalked off, shouting 'You have killed that man! Come to my study!' Fan, covered in mud, dusted herself down, highly embarrassed and convinced that she would be instantly dispatched home – only relieved that she had not wasted £300 on a uniform.

In the dragon's study, Fan stood to attention as instructed, thumbs in line with skirt seams. This was made more difficult because the dragon's Pekinese was snapping away at her skirt hem. 'Will you stand still?' said the dragon, with a fierce look. Looking back, Fan feels she was way out of her depth: shehad failed. She would not be transferred to the Red Cross, which ran the ambulances that were driven by FANY drivers. Her heart was in her boots. After a pause the dragon spoke. 'I can get you another job, but I can't give you details. You must report to a restaurant in Baker Street – and you must buy your uniform before your interview.' Fan was told that she would be approached by an English officer with the major's crown on his epaulette. He would say, 'Simpson, follow me.'

Winifred had passed the driving test, but decided she did not want to proceed with Red Cross ambulance driving. Instead she was sent to Bletchley Park, where the Enigma code was cracked: just about the most secret establishment of all. Fan, however, was not to know that she exactly fitted the requirements for a staff job with the newly formed SOE. Even so, off she went to Lilywhites to purchase the full set of dress and working uniform, including an enormous 'British Warm' officer's greatcoat, which she never wore: it was too heavy! Her great adventure was about to begin.

CHAPTER 9

The Secret War

'I fear no foe, I fawn no friend, I loathe not life, nor
dread my end.' *William Shakespeare*

F
an was now plunged into a strange and alien world of
clandestine skulduggery. Nothing was the same again, and
nothing was as it seemed. After reporting to the restaurant
in Baker Street, in full uniform, having been instructed to
tell no one where she was going, for the next four years she had no
existence outside the SOE. It was to be her family, and Gubbins her
mentor and surrogate father.

A bemused Fan was collected by the major and delivered to 64
Baker Street, where she was handed over to a transport officer. He
led her to an office occupied by a colonel. Completely bewildered,
Fan had no idea who this was, although she was immediately struck
by the easy charm and civility of the tall, dashingly handsome
Grenadier Guards colonel. It was in fact the urbane Douglas Dodds-
Parker, who like Gubbins became in time a close friend. Dodds-
Parker had taken part in courses run by Gubbins, and by this stage
was a key figure at SOE HQ, the so-called Inter Services Research
Bureau. He was responsible for the introduction of FANYs to SOE:
some took on staff jobs while others were used as operations room

personnel or on secretarial duties. It is likely that Fan was one of the earliest such recruits. Some of the FANYs recruited by SOE had been employed as secretaries at Baker Street before the war, when it had been the headquarters of Marks & Spencer, and these civilian entrants along with later recruits direct from FANY were required to do fifteen days' basic training. After 1943 this took place at Overthorpe Hall, near Banbury.

Fan had only received brief training in Norfolk before being failed as an ambulance driver and dispatched to Baker Street. At this point in the development of SOE security training seems to have been minimal, and based very largely on trust and honour. Fan was simply told to tell no one where she was or what she was doing for the rest of the war. To start with this was not difficult, since she had no idea what she was to do or what the role of SOE actually was.

By 1943 security training provided brutal and terrifying reminders of the lives that were put at stake if any operational information was leaked by FANYs, especially those working on wireless and coding roles, and helping to run hundreds of agents throughout Europe. In her account, Margaret Pawley tells us that two young recruits were so terrified by their training that they were afraid to look out of the plane window en route to Italy! At least Fan was spared that: she developed a remarkable capacity for coping with every experience, however bizarre.

The first period of Fan's service was defined by hectic confusion, with her usual share of personal disasters. On her first day Dodds-Parker told her he needed a driver immediately, and that the staff office would tell her where to find the car. Her instruction was to go to the rear of the building, where she would find a large Humber (a model much favoured as staff cars); this she was to take down to Marylebone Road to a block of flats with an underground garage, where she should fill up with petrol before returning to Baker Street to pick up the colonel. Unfamiliar with this large and unwieldy vehicle, with a leather bench seat, little Fan lost control on the ramp and hit a concrete pillar. As the resident mechanic remarked, 'You finished that one off!' In a state of panic, Fan trudged back to Baker Street to report to the transport officer. To her surprise he was unfazed. Instead of hauling her up on a disciplinary charge, he simply remarked that there was another car available, but that, since she was 'not very big', she should take a walk up Baker Street to a furniture store to buy a couple of cushions before she picked it up, so she could reach the controls more easily. Fan bought a very large pillow, and reported back for duty.

As she quaked in her shoes out came Dodds-Parker, who said, 'Take me to Station 12, and be there in two hours!' Fan must have looked confused since he added, 'Just go, I'll direct.' Their destination turned out to be near St Albans, where Fan had nothing to do but wait, happy that everybody had been incredibly kind to her, despite another disastrous start. This impression (and that of a distinctive English amateurishness) stayed with her all her life. Despite the intimate and claustrophobic atmosphere of the SOE, at home and abroad, she never saw or experienced any hint of sexual impropriety or harassment, despite being a pretty young woman, widowed, lonely and far from home.

The hectic and unpredictable nature of Fan's duties as a young staff driver for senior officers soon taught her the first rule of SOE life: always go to work with a clean nightie, undies and shirt, and a toothbrush. She could be required to go anywhere at any time, often driving unfamiliar routes at night in the blackout, with headlamps cut down with tape to a one inch beam.

A few days later Fan met her friend and mentor to be, Brigadier Gubbins, for the first time. His regular driver was off ill. When she was sent to his office his first words were, 'Oh, are you very kindly going to drive me?' Halfway down Baker Street, hyperactive as always, Gubbins announced that he wanted to drive instead. Feeling a little hurt, but assuming that he must have heard of her earlier disasters, Fan made to pull in, but Gubbins said, 'Don't stop, just move up,' and proceeded to slide along the bench seat (it was a column-change Humber), urging her to climb over him while he took the wheel – without stopping!

Her next encounter with her eccentric boss was when she was detailed to drive him to an urgent meeting at the War Office in Whitehall. As she raced south she was stopped by a diligent police constable and issued with a speeding fine. Gubbins's only comment was, 'Oh dear, that was rather a shame. Perhaps I should pay.'

A little later Fan had to drive Gubbins to the Polish station, where escaped Polish servicemen were training to go into the field as agents in occupied Poland. Presumably some news was filtering through of atrocities committed by the occupying German forces, since Gubbins remarked in his brusque Scottish manner, 'Morale is low.' As they drove through the blacked-out countryside late at night, after a fourteen hour day at Baker Street, Gubbins announced that he proposed to raise morale by teaching the Polish agents Scottish dancing – which he proceeded to do with Fan's assistance, at 2am! It didn't do Fan's morale much good, and who knows what the Poles thought of it, but Gubbins enjoyed himself!

Soon after this episode, Fan was transferred to operator room duties at Baker Street, probably to her relief. The ops room was a reinforced bombproof concrete structure within the walls of the existing building. Here wireless operators, mostly FANYs, were responsible for sending and receiving coded messages to agents in the field.

The amazing courage and fortitude of agents of both sexes, and many nationalities, is well recorded elsewhere. Suffice to say that the Wireless Telegraphy (WT) operators among them, hampered by a suitcase full of very heavy equipment, were at constant risk. It was clear, therefore, that the WT girls in the ops room carried a great responsibility for many lives. It was essential that incoming coded messages were exactly recorded on paper, and that outgoing traffic was accurate and properly coded.

In late 1941 Bingham was requested by SOE to train FANYs as wireless operators, in addition to those training as coders in enciphering and deciphering signals traffic. Over 100 FANYs were so trained in 1944, and later posted to the Mediterranean. Some were selected by Gamwell and Bingham on the basis that they had musical ability, which was thought to give them a special aptitude. The training took place at Station 52 (Thorne Park), and originally was based on the Playfair code, which was later superceded by Double Transition. Both involved the use of lines from poems or single words, and they were rendered obsolete by One Time Pads, which were considered unbreakable. Here the words of the message itself were not used: each letter was replaced by one from a list that was used only once. Main line traffic between London and base stations such as Algiers or Cairo was in a numerical code from the War Office 'book'. The critical feature of all codes was the use of two sorts of check in every message. This was to ensure that the message was genuine and that the wireless operator in the field had not been lost and replaced by the Gestapo. One was a bluff check to confuse the Germans; the other was genuine. It is not clear whether failure to ensure that this system was observed led to the turning of more than one circuit, or whether this was, as is sometimes claimed, a deliberate sacrifice to confuse the Germans about the likely whereabouts of the D-Day invasion.

FANY wireless operators underwent more rigorous training at Station 54A Fawley. Those who were unable to achieve the speed and accuracy required to become WT operators were moved to related ops room and HQ jobs, as coders, registry clerks (who copied and distributed signals) and teleprinter switchboard operators. The wireless operator course took four months and involved reaching a twenty-plus words per minute transmission speed, a vital skill for those in the field who had fleeting and dangerous moments in which to transmit an urgent message before being traced by the enemy, who had detector vans. Of course all WT business was transmitted in Morse, well known to ex-Girl Guides but difficult to learn from scratch at speed.

Since Fan was such an early recruit she never undertook the formal training, and when she was moved into the operations room it was in the role as coordinator of 'triage'. A large map of Europe covered one wall, around which flags representing agents and circuits (networks of agents) could be moved. Numerous WT operators took and transmitted messages, while Fan sorted incoming messages by importance, selecting those of most significance and taking them to Gubbins or Dodds-Parker, or Gubbins's aide, Margaret Jackson. Return messages were taken by Fan to be coded and transmitted. This role involved incredibly long hours – sixteen to eighteen hour days in artificial light, working at intense speed. There were no days off or weekends, and after a few months Fan was unsurprisingly exhausted. One day Gubbins remarked, 'God, you look tired! I'm going to transfer you to Cornwall.'

CHAPTER 10

High Stakes in Cornwall

*'I held my tongue, and spake nothing: I kept
silence, yea, even from good words; but it was
pain and grief to me.'*
Psalm 39

Having served her apprenticeship at 64 Baker Street, Fan embarked on a more directly active role. The SOE station in Cornwall was to bring her much nearer the real war in one sense, despite freeing her from the ever-present threat of bombing.

In August 1940 a paper to the CEO/SOE suggested that SO2 should as 'one of its principal tasks recruit a carefully selected body of saboteurs operating exclusively against objectives on or near coasts at short notice, at widely separated points'. On 18 March 1941 Gubbins minuted thus: 'all the various parties of men who we are now training may well have to be landed by sea as no other means exist'. As we have seen already, SOE was regarded with suspicion and real dislike by senior figures in all the regular services and in intelligence, as well as the civil service and even government. Gubbins seems to have got on better with politicians (with the exception of Anthony Eden) than with generals and admirals, and

SOE would not have survived without the patronage of Churchill himself.

Later in the war, despite continuing opposition, the normal transport link with occupied Europe for agents was aircraft and parachute. At this stage, so soon after Dunkirk and with the Battle of Britain raging overhead, extra aircraft were out of the question, yet Gubbins and SOE had to find some way of inspiring the French resistance movement to hamper the occupying German army in every way possible. Potential agents from the ranks of escaped French servicemen or civilians, or bilingual English citizens, had to be trained in wireless telegraphy, coding, the use of weapons, disguise and so on; then they had to be placed in northern France.

Decisions had to be made about the areas SOE could operate in. As usual there were problems of inter-service rivalry. The intelligence services managed to impose a complete veto on SOE operations between the Channel Islands and St Nazaire, which excluded SOE from the areas most suitable for their small-scale operations. Only a small number of the Breton beaches targeted by Gubbins were available. SOE operations were later hampered by the intervention of the Royal Navy, which insisted on overall control of all seagoing operations, imposing a coordinator on SOE for this field of operations in 1943.

By late 1941 Gubbins had established a training base and departure point on the Helford river in Cornwall, west of Falmouth, and was investigating various types of sea transport. Submarines appeared to be the ideal choice, but were rarely available and were not particularly successful. Fast and small surface craft such as Motor Gun Boats (MGBs) were suitable, given the primitive state of German radar, but again were rarely available. Much lower risk, if slower and not very comfortable, were fishing boats of Breton design.

As early as October 1940, Commander Gerry Holdsworth (RN) was setting up a fleet of small craft. His first vessel was a Seaplane tender, which had limited space and speed. Deciding that fishing boats would be more useful, he managed to get hold of a tunnyman, a long liner and a motor trawler, all of French origin. These vessels had the capacity to hold 5 tons of stores, and could manage 7 or 8 knots. Five more similar vessels were acquired later. The nearby country house of Lady Sears (of the Sears retail group) was requisitioned as a training centre, as it had a garden running down to the river where the fishing vessels were based.

Fan was sent along with Commander McIntosh (RN) to establish the training centre in 1942. She was initially based in a hotel in Falmouth while Lady Sears moved out. The establishment, of which Gerry Holdsworth was the CO, consisted of Fan and a few Army troops, who were guards and cooks. At any time three or four agents in training were resident, before departure for Brittany. During this period Fan was effectively staff officer, in charge of secretarial and domestic arrangements. Once the station was established she reverted to the triage duties that she had carried out at Baker Street, although she continued to have a variety of odd jobs thrown her way. Fan decoded incoming messages from Baker Street and coded replies. These messages were sent via normal BBC radio programmes, even news bulletins. Internal security was critical, and a strict rule was that nothing should be left lying about on paper. As the number of staff increased it was essential to ensure that nothing was accidentally leaked about the activities of the station, or its whereabouts, by girls of lower rank who still had family, friends or boyfriends – and tried to send postcards after taking a bus to remote villages. All these matters of security fell to Fan, who was effectively personal assistant to Holdsworth, and very much the 'conscientious prefect' as she puts it; in reality the power behind the throne. Senior SOE officers were selected because they were proven men of action and lateral thinkers, rather than able adjutants with administrative skills. This is why Fan was so important to Gubbins, Holdsworth and Dodds-Parker.

Another role that fell to Fan was looking after the needs of the agents in training. This must have drawn on her good humour, sympathy and empathy: they all knew that they were embarking on a journey that involved great danger and the probability of a terrible death if they were betrayed or captured. Fan had found it more difficult at Baker Street, where she had been required to take agents for dinner on the evening before they were due to fly.

Despite the chaos, and the high stakes, Fan's life was not all harrowing and stressful. During Fan's tour in Cornwall, Holdsworth received a message from the War Office that they had graciously decided FANYs would be paid an honorarium of 2s 6d (half a crown) per week. At this time Fan was also promoted to the Army equivalent rank of corporal. 'Let's have a party,' said Holdsworth. 'Fan, go down to Falmouth and get us some champagne.' This was a daunting assignment in 1942, which Fan managed with her usual style. An excellent time was had by all, and at this point in her story Fan always reflects with amazement that all ranks were always 'perfect gentlemen'.

Fan was in Cornwall for about six months before receiving a message from FANY HQ asking for volunteers: FANY officers who were willing to be posted to stations unknown. Fan was ready for a change and volunteered, even though the message made it plain that she would end up in a war zone somewhere. This was unlikely to be behind enemy lines in Fan's case, as she was not fluent in French. Pearl Harbor had brought America into the war by this stage, and an assault on French North Africa was being prepared: Fan was not aware of this.

She was instructed to take a large staff car back to London and report to 64 Baker Street for further orders. As usual, potential disaster resulted from her encounter with a large and unyielding Humber, for which her diminutive stature rendered her unsuitable: the controls of cars in those days were not designed for women. The trip from Cornwall to London of 200 miles on trunk roads was long and tiring for a young woman exhausted by months of unremitting work. While crossing Salisbury Plain she dropped off to sleep, and woke with a start to find a high stone wall bearing down on her. She slammed on the brakes to find herself only a foot away from the wall. As she remarks, she must have a guardian angel!

When Fan had returned the car she went home to her shared flat behind Hyde Park to await orders. She was 'only afraid of bombs and not people' as she walked across the park in the dark, often late at night.

CHAPTER 11

Fighting Back

'For now sits expectation in the air …'
William Shakespeare

The successful landing in Algeria of the Eighth Army under General Montgomery's Desert Rats marked a turning point in the war. England was still under the cosh of German bombing, while losses of shipping convoys in the North Atlantic to the U-boat campaign continued. But at last we had gone on the offensive and soon American forces would join us. We no longer stood alone.

By now Gubbins had created a network of agents in France and elsewhere in occupied Western Europe. But in 1941 SOE's performance was not seen as satisfactory by their political masters. Some circuits of agents had been penetrated and destroyed. Hugh Dalton expressed disappointment at the time spent in training and preparation, and the cost of it. The only outright success was the seizure of the 7600 ton Italian liner *Duchessa d'Aosta*, which had sought refuge in a neutral port, Fernando Po in Spanish West Africa. This remarkable feat was accomplished by Major Gus March-Phillips and Captain J.G. Appleyard, using a fishing smack out of Poole Harbour.

In 1942 Charles Hambro replaced Sir Frank Nelson as political head of SOE. Thanks to Dalton, Nelson and Gladwyn Jebb SOE's standing in Whitehall, and relations between Baker Street and the chiefs of staff, were much improved. The Air Ministry was still unconvinced, and hampered efforts to make more aircraft available to SOE. By June 1942 SOE had just ten Halifax bombers on hand, so missions in Poland and Czechoslovakia were minimal.

At this point Dalton was moved sideways, to become President of the Board of Trade. Gubbins was grateful for his support, but was well aware of Dalton's unpopularity in the Cabinet. His successor, the Earl of Selbourne, made a good impression on Gubbins, and the feeling was mutual. The entry of America and Russia into the war made the prospect of reinvading Europe more likely – at which point SOEs' ability to subvert German defences with operations behind their lines would come into its own. SOE had survived several serious attempts to disband it, and now its role could go beyond sabotage and subversion to the creation of patriot armies, able to rise up against the occupying forces at the same time as Europe was invaded. This was the dream that had preoccupied both Gubbins and Churchill since 1940.

By summer 1942 the Allies had agreed the division of responsibility for special operations: Western Europe was shared between SOE and OSS (America's secret service); the Balkans, Middle East and West Africa were to be Britain's responsibility; America was to be responsible for China, Korea, Finland, the Pacific and North Africa. It was the latter that interested Gubbins. SOEs' activities in North Africa were to be in support of the military invasion, Operation Torch, for which he had only three months to prepare.

Operation Torch was to be led by the Americans from AFHQ (Allied Forces HQ). Colonel Munn was selected by Gubbins to be SOE's man at AFHQ; Douglas Dodds-Parker was to be CO of the SOE team to be established near Algiers.

Fan's orders came a few days later. She was instructed to report to Euston station the next Sunday evening, along with ten other FANY officers from SOE. They were told nothing of where they were going, other than to join the night train to Liverpool. On arrival, on a cold, dark night early in 1942, they were transferred to a troopship.

The troopship was a stripped-down cruise liner, which was extremely overcrowded with 3000 troops (reinforcements for the Eighth Army at Algiers) and just eleven FANY officers. The girls were given strict instructions to fraternise (but not too eagerly!) with all ranks, not just officers. They were accommodated in two large cabins on the upper deck, six in one, five in the other, where they slept on the floor.

The English Channel and Western Approaches were infested with U-boats, and within reach of German aircraft from the French coast. A direct passage down the Bay of Biscay and the Spanish and Portuguese coasts was impossible, therefore, so the troopship had to join a convoy en route for America. They enjoyed an uneventful voyage as far as American territorial waters, where the troopship turned east and made a direct run for the Straits of Gibraltar and the Mediterranean.

U-boats were extremely active in this sea area, and not many hours ahead of Fan's troopship another vessel bound on the same errand, carrying over 200 Queen Alexandra's Nursing Corps, was sunk by a U-boat with all lives lost. As the Eighth Army fought its way east there were inevitably many casualties, and the loss of these nurses was felt by the field hospitals in Algiers. Fan knew nothing of this until later, but remembers the last part of the journey as a very scary experience.

To her relief they arrived safely in Algiers. The SOE station was to be located in a holiday complex originally built by the sea for rich French Algerians. Club de Pines, 15 miles east of Algiers, was surrounded by fields and pinewoods. Commandeered for SOE, it was given the codename Massingham. The villas had been stripped of their furniture and were therefore primitive as accommodation. Larger buildings were used as a dining area and as offices, including a large office for the CO, Douglas Dodds-Parker, for whom Fan was to work. Another large villa was the signals office, where the other FANYs were to work. The girls were to share villas, sleeping on camp beds, with ammunition boxes as their bedside cabinets. Working dress was linen skirt and khaki cotton shirt, because of the heat. There was no danger of indiscipline among the young FANY officers, thanks to the presence of Phyllis Bingham – the dragon lady – as senior officer.

As always Fan's life was dominated by hard work, receiving incoming messages from the signals office and decoding them. Among routine matters was some seriously 'hush-hush' work, which involved typing and coding messages between Dodds-Parker and Churchill. These were to do with the plans that were being developed with Eisenhower for D-Day: the reinvasion of Europe, which was still a year away. The idea was to organise a hoax landing at Marseilles just before the landings in northern France, to make the Germans think that the invasion was about to happen on the beaches of southern France. This clandestine operation was probably inspired by the success of Operation Mincemeat, immediately before the invasion of North Africa, when the body of a Welsh tramp was covertly acquired and recreated as a British officer carrying fake secret documents, complete with a personal history and appropriate documents to prove his authenticity. The fake major was deposited by submarine off the Spanish south coast, and his documents, indicating the intention of the Allies to invade Greece and the Balkans rather than Sicily, successfully deceived the Germans – ensuring the success of Operation Torch, the invasion of North Africa, just before Fan arrived.

Despite the pressure of hard work, there were hilarious incidents as well. One fine day Bingham gave the girls a half-day off to relax on the beach, have a swim and do a little sunbathing. While they were on the sand in their swimsuits, Bingham suddenly said, 'Keep still, girls!' She had spotted an incoming Messerschmitt 109 coming in low, and feared they were to be strafed by its machine guns. Fortunately the pilot was distracted by the sight of all the scantily dressed girls, and never realised he could have wiped out the signals and coding capacity of the Allied Forces – or perhaps he was just a gentleman.

On another occasion, senior American officers at AFHQ needed to be won over to the idea of SOE, so Dodds-Parker suggested the FANY should do a can-can as part of an evening's light entertainment: a local variety theatre in Algiers had costumes. Fan was horrified and very shy. She had never been on stage before, let alone in the front row of the can-can!

The pretty young FANY officers were required very occasionally to attend official balls, dinners, and so on at AFHQ in

Algiers, as escorts to the senior officers. It was on one such occasion that Fan and her ten colleagues had the privilege of meeting King George VI when he made a secret visit to Massingham, while Fan was acting as escort to Dodds-Parker. During this period Fan also met Harold Macmillan, minister for the Middle East, and also Duff Cooper, from 1943 the British government's liaison with the Free French. When in conference they used Dodds-Parker's villa, and Fan had to make sure things went smoothly.

In addition to her decoding work for Dodds-Parker, Fan was chosen as one of four FANYs to do a nightshift turn and turn about, manning the wireless receiver to pick up messages from agents in Italy who were searching for Mussolini with a view to assassinating him. Fan found that she struggled to stay awake, and could not understand why the other girls did better. When she asked them for their secret, they said 'black coffee and fags'. So Fan took up cigarettes, which have sustained her right through to her ninety-seventh year (along with vodka and whisky).

One day Bingham issued the weekly ration of chocolate, cigarettes and alcohol. Fan left some chocolate for later on her ammunition box bedside table, only to wake up later to find herself face to face with a large rat – at which she screamed. On another occasion she was walking from the office back to her quarters with the girls, and the sky suddenly went black. An enormous cloud of locusts descended on them, completely covering them, getting into clothes, hair and everywhere. Mad panic ensued as they dashed back to the office to clean themselves up, before returning to quarters – where they found everything covered in locusts, beds and all. A big clean-up job was required. The outcome for the local inhabitants was tragic, since the crops in the surrounding fields had been completely stripped. Fan seems to have been much more frightened of rats, locusts, spiders and so on than anything the Germans could throw at her.

By the end of 1943 the North African campaign had been completed, and the Allies had fought their way across Sicily before landing at Salerno. Two FANYs were chosen to join Dodds-Parker in the Naples area, and Fan was one of them; the other was her bosom friend, Leonora Railton. Life was about to become even more exciting.

CHAPTER 12

The Italian Campaign

'And all the things of beauty burn
With flames of evil ecstasy.'
Lionel Johnson

Fan would have known little at the time of the political turbulence in 1943 that again threatened the very existence of SOE. The defeat of the Germans at Stalingrad and the rapid advance of Soviet forces brought out the inherent suspicion and fear of Communism that had been obscured for two years. The predominant role of SOE in fomenting 'patriot' movements in the Balkans, especially Tito's Communist organisation, worried both the British and American governments, while OSS, the American equivalent to SOE, resented British dominance in that area of operations.

As Churchill convalesced after an attack of pneumonia, he fretted that the Italian campaign being waged by the Fifth and Eighth Armies was stagnating. Meanwhile discussion continued about the relative priority of the Italian campaign and Operation Overlord, the invasion of France. In May 1943 at the Tehran Conference, America, Britain and Russia, Roosevelt, Churchill and Stalin agreed that the latter was the more important, together with a landing in southern France. Churchill felt that it was necessary and possible to speed up the advance through Italy with Operation Shingle, a two-pronged attack that would include landings at Anzio. This would draw German forces from the Western Europe and Russian fronts.

The dispatch of General Eisenhower to England to prepare for Overlord left the Mediterranean theatre under British control. General Sir Harold Alexander remained commander-in-chief, since he was thought to have mastered the art 'of managing the Americans'. General Mark Clark commanded the American Fifth Army, fighting on the western side of Italy, while General Sir Oliver Leese was to command the British Eighth Army on the eastern side of Italy. Meanwhile Churchill sought to delay the proposed Overlord landings (D-Day) in France by a month.

By 8 January 1944 Clark could write in his diary, 'Shingle is on!' and 22 January 1944 was decided upon as the start date. Beachhead landings were to take place at Anzio and Nettuno, where the former port and the beaches were suitable. The landings would involve a combined American and British force, VI Corps, under American General Lucas, who had serious misgivings about the sufficiency of his force for the job. Meanwhile the Eighth Army under General Lucas was to advance towards Cassino on the road north towards Rome.

Lucas was old, stolid and methodical, while Clark was extrovert and eager to be first to Rome. He disliked taking orders from Alexander, the paternalistic British officer. Cassino was to be pivotal in the attempt to breach the German defensive Gustav Line. Anglo-American rivalry was damaging to the Allied efforts, causing Churchill to cable Wilson on 18 January, 'No one is keener than I on working with the Americans in closest comradeship. I am however anxious that Operation Shingle should be a joint concern, and not, as may be represented a purely American victory … It will lead to bitterness in Great Britain when the claim is stridently put forward, as it surely will be, that the Americans have taken Rome.' Churchill's fears were justified, and American versions of this campaign did indeed claim that the Americans were first to Rome. As we shall see, Fan knows this to be untrue.

On 9 September 1943 Eighth Army HQ moved up to Naples. SOE HQ remained at Massingham, but Dodds-Parker relocated to

SOE/HQ (Med)/LIASON, codename Speedwell, at a village near Naples. This unit was intended to manage more efficiently the extensive SOE (M) undercover work with resistance fighters among the population of Italy, across the Adriatic Sea in the Balkans and further north. Much of the work was still to be done at Massingham, but Dodds-Parker decided to take a skeleton staff of two FANY officers with him: Fan and Leonora.

Dodds-Parker flew to Naples on 9 September 1943; Fan and Leonora travelled by Italian fishing boat. This involved a forty-eight -hour journey in extremely uncomfortable conditions in the care of a rather licentious fisherman. Apart from the discomfort, squalor and danger, the two girls were worried about using the primitive toilet, each having to keep guard while the other used the facilities. Dodds -Parker met the girls with a Jeep on the dockside. He had already commandeered a villa on the outskirts of Naples in a district called the Orange Grove.

The SOE advance party consisted of Dodds-Parker, Fan and Leonora, and three private soldiers as guards and drivers. As they drove out of Naples, Fan, as ever practical, asked Dodds-Parker, 'What have you done about food?' He replied, 'Oh, nothing'. It was a good question but a bad answer. The retreating Germans had taken or destroyed all food supplies, and the local population were literally starving. After their uncomfortable boat journey Fan and Leonora were not only dirty and dishevelled, but were also extremely hungry. As they drove up the winding road in the hills east of Naples, shortly before they arrived at the villa Fan noticed a sign at the roadside for the 58th Anti Aircraft Battalion. Once they had arrived at their new home, Fan volunteered to walk back there to scrounge some rations. With her usual style she approached the squaddie at the gate and asked to see the commanding officer. The guard was completely thrown by the sight of a young English female officer in a uniform bearing the FANY insignia, which he had never seen before. He responded, 'No you can't. Who are you, anyway? I've never seen that badge before.' 'OK,' said Fan, 'then can I see your second in command?' 'No!' 'I've got six Brits up the road who need feeding. We need a ration allowance,' said Fan, refusing to move. The guard went off to search for the officer, rather intimidated by this tiny but assertive young woman.

Finally the second in command came out to see what was going on. 'Who are you?' To which a rather exasperated Fan replied, 'This is a FANY badge. We need a ration allowance for six. Can you include us on your strength?' 'Don't know. I'll have to go and see the colonel.' By this time Fan was becoming seriously stroppy, replying firmly, 'Can you see six Brits starve?'

A little while later he returned. 'Colonel Hewlett says that if you're really British we can help.' So off he went off to the kitchen, bringing out a sergeant who was sent with a squaddie to fetch some ration boxes for the next two days, after which they were to be included on the 58th's strength for rations.

Fan walked back to the villa with her boxes of rations, and they set about eating 'like vultures'. As Fan remarks, Dodds-Parker was 'a brilliant soldier but not a practical man', so this escapade was a lifeline. After all, an army marches on its stomach.

As usual Fan's duties, in addition to decoding messages, included running the villa and the office, but she was not allowed to drive in the war zone. Unsurprisingly, even among the heartbreak and rubble of a defeated enemy, there were comic incidents. On the second night in the villa Fan and Leonora retired to bed, under their mosquito nets. Suddenly they woke in horror, screaming their heads off: they were being bitten to death by bedbugs, which had climbed up the mosquito net and dropped onto them. The squaddie on guard rushed in, rifle at the ready, to be faced by two panicking female officers, stark naked and covered in bedbugs and spots of blood. 'Can you do something about these mosquito nets?' screamed Fan. The well-trained but embarrassed squaddie averted his eyes, ripped off the nets, stood to attention, rifle shouldered and eyes still averted, did a smart turn and marched out. He took the mosquito nets to the bathroom and dunked them in a bath of water. The girls returned to bed; the bedbugs had committed suicide in the bath and caused no more problems. But they awoke covered with bedbug and mosquito bites. At breakfast Dodds-Parker ordered new mosquito nets to be put up, and the girls never had problems with bedbugs and mosquitoes again.

Vera Aungiers (aka Fan Craig) c. 1939

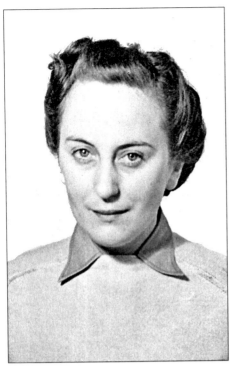

In 1941-2 before joining FANY.

General Colin Gubbins, Director SOE 1941-45, entering the War Office. Fan started as his driver. then in Coding at SOE HQ at 64 Baker Street, ending the war as his ADC. A lifelong friend, he gave her away at her wedding in 1945.

ENROLMENT FORM

WOMEN'S TRANSPORT SERVICE
(F. A. N. Y.)
President : H.R.H. Princess Alice, Countess of Athlone.

Headquarters : 10, Lower Grosvenor Place, London, S.W.1.

Declaration :

To be sworn in the presence of an Officer of the Corps.

(1) I* *Vera Muriel Aungier*
hereby declare that I am a British subject, and that I will be faithful and bear
true allegiance to His Majesty King George VI, his Heirs and Successors.

(2) I declare my loyalty to the Women's Transport Service (F.A.N.Y.), and I will faithfully
uphold the Constitution and Standing Orders of the Corps as laid down by
the Commandant and Council of the Corps, or as amended by them ; and will
carry out such orders as may be issued to me by the approved Commandant
or by duly appointed officers acting under her authority.

(3) I am willing to serve at home or overseas, as required, in times of National Emergency.
(*If for Home Service only, the recruit must strike out the words "or overseas"
and initial the alteration before the officer witnessing her declaration*).

(4) I understand that the Corps reserves the right to dismiss me through the authority
laid down in the Constitution and Standing Orders of the Corps, without reason
assigned.

Signed this *17th* day of *December* 19 *41*

(signature) *Vera Aungier*

(address) *15 Harwood Gat, Putney S.W.15.*

in the presence of *Elizabeth Hunt*

Rank or authority *Lieutenant and Adjutant*
WTS/FANY

(*) *Vera Muriel Aungier*
having signed the above Declaration, is hereby enrolled a member of **the**
WOMEN'S TRANSPORT SERVICE (F.A.N.Y.),

Elizabeth Hunt Officer in charge of
Lieutenant and Adjutant WTS/FANY Section.

Acceptance of Enrolment *M. Maria ...*
Officer-in-Charge, H.Q.

Date *14/12/41*
*FULL NAME OF MEMBER.

Fan's enrolment form or FANY, December 1941.

EH/MA

F 11702
08/310/13

September 3rd, 1942

Dear Aungiers,

It is with great pleasure that I am instructed by the Commanding Officer W.T.S./.F.A.N.Y. to inform you that you have been promoted to Lance-Corporal, with effect from 22.8.42.

I trust that you will enjoy your new duties, and I know the Corps will look to you to carry out your responsibilities in a through and understanding manner, both from the work and personnel point of view.

Yours sincerely,

Elizabeth Hunt

Captain and Adjutant.
W.T.S./.F.A.N.Y.

Mrs. Aungiers,
Room 98. Horseguards.
Whitehall. S.W.1.

Fan is promoted to lance-corporal, 22 Feb 1942.

Fan finds time to relax with Dodds-Parker and an American General.

Colonel Dodds-Parker relaxing at home.

Dodds-Parker stands as MP for Banbury in the 1945 general election. He would win the seat for the Conservatives.

Major General Stawell. CO SOE in Italy, 1944, for whom Fan became ADC on promotion to Captain (the equivalent army rank to Major.

Fan's only appearance as a can-can girl in a show for visiting dignitaries at Massingham, 1943.

Fan relaxes with a colleague in Cairo and visits the pyramids.

Returning to Naples via Athens—photo to remind Fan that
Greece was the cradle of European civilisation, despite the
distress so evident during her flying visit.

London.
2/10/44

My dear Vera,

Congratulations on being made a captain — Comdr Henderson told me about it when she came to see me this morning. I hear you are to work for the General, as being the most efficient Fany in the lmed! I'm sure you'll enjoy it.

Douglas has arrived home and I have seen him for just a moment. I wonder how you like Italy after your very nice place at Algiers — it was always heartening to visit Massingham, such grand spirit in the place; I miss it a lot, specially as being our first off-shoot from the firm to go out from England.

Massingham is still working for me here, and Col Barry as chief of staff. The work seems to be as much as ever, especially as we have the future to try & plan for, & have many things to struggle against.

Send me a line & let me know all your news. Best of luck to you, & to Jane & Joan if they are about.

Yours ever,

Colin G.

From Dodds-Parker to Fan on her promotion to Captain and ADC to Major General Stawell, 1943.

The villa, belonging to Baron Albert de Schonen, French SOE officer, which was lent to General Stawell, Fan and Jof Hewitt (later to be Fan's husband) for a brief break in Summer, 1944.

Monte Casino after the great battle through which Fan and
General Stawell drove hours after the Germans retreated.

Notes for A.D.C.

1. Keep appointments and give me daily list if necessary.
2. Make tour arrangements, Tour reports.
3. Keep lists of people whom I should know and warn me when I am going to meet.
4. See that correspondence comes to me in proper form, and that I see all telegrams etc that I should.
5. See that anybody has access to me who has something of interest to say.
6. See that Tps and OR's going into the field on coming out see me if whenever it can be arranged.
7. See that I am told of casualties in the field and find out particulars of next of kin etc so that I can write or that one unit concerned writes letters of condolence.
8. Fix up social engagements. See that people I should entertain are invited – Fix up seating at dinner etc –
9. Give orders for car and make necessary arrangements for Cpl Howe.
10. Keep in touch with F.A.N.Y. daily we meet at out stations and see that F.A.N.Y. Hq are au fait with conditions –
11. Keep handover & S.O.N. in touch with my movements
12. Remind me to keep C.D. informed of major policy matters.
13. Keep accounts of expenses incurred on firm's behalf and reclaim for Whiting.
14. Keep diary of my movements
15. Generally bring to my notice unofficially all matters that require attention, noticed from your own observation and mentioned to you by others.
16. Keep in touch with all that goes on in the office so that you can give an intelligent answer on my behalf, or refer matters if appropriate still office in my absence.
17. Do secretarial work in absence of P.A.
18.

On her appointment as General Stawell's ADC, he gave her this job description.

Fan enjoying happy retirement at the age of eighty-five.

CHAPTER 13
Naples and Promotion

'Crabbed Age and Youth
Cannot live together ...'
William Shakespeare

The villa at Orange Grove continued as SOE HQ for SOE (M) (Special Operations Mediterranean) for some months. This period was to be the most exciting of the war for Fan. The invasion of Italy had prompted the country to sign an armistice on 8 September 1943; the surrender negotiations had been handled by Mary McIntyre, a FANY colleague. The German occupying force was increased and the regime became to oppress the Italian population.

While Dodds-Parker and his small team remained resident at the Naples villa, the operational HQ for SOE (M) was established at Bari, near Brindisi, in the Palazzo Albertonza, on the east coast of Italy, the only available airfield. Dodds-Parker had arrived courtesy of British Sixth Airborne Division together with his motorbike at Brindisi, where he was met by Gerry Holdsworth who had travelled by sea. Gerry had commandeered some suitable buildings at Monopoli. The new HQ was codenamed Maryland, and signals traffic continued to be routed through Massingham until given independence by order of General Gubbins in October 1943.

The FANY mess and offices were in Casa Camicia, via Bixio 192 and adjacent buildings. The FANY contingent that was to staff the operational HQ arrived after a hazardous journey by lorry along the North African coast and by infantry landing craft across the Mediterranean.

Gerry Holdsworth set up his office at Bari, together with two FANY assistants, Ensign Gundred Grogan and Ruth Hermon-Smith. Fan of course had arrived some weeks earlier, and remained at the Naples villa with Dodds-Parker.

The function of SOE (M) was to run agents and patriots behind German lines, with the aim of creating chaos and destruction by sabotage both in Italy and Balkan regions. Allied Forces HQ had moved from Algiers to Caserta near Naples, where it occupied the Palace of Caserta.

Apart from her routine administrative duties at the villa, Fan continued work with the coding and relay of messages to and from Dodds-Parker to London, many of which related to the planning of the D-Day landings. Dodds-Parker was preparing a report for Churchill, 'Imaginative planning for a landing in the South of France'. Fan recalls that Dodds-Parker's proposed plan was for a landing at Marseilles followed by an advance in a north-easterly direction to Klagenfurt on the Rhine, where the advance was to turn east, presumably to link up with the Fifth and Eighth Armies advancing north through Italy.

Fan was also required to liaise with AFHQ, ferrying messages to and from Dodds-Parker. Fan commandeered the very bad-tempered Italian gardener who lived in the lodge gate cottage at the villa as her driver, since she was not allowed to drive in a war zone. Most of the 250 FANY staff who were employed at Massingham in Algiers remained there, while the AFHQ administrative staff consisted of thirty-eight ATS personnel.

Even at the height of a chaotic period of the war there were opportunities for a little innocent fun. The arrival at Caserta of the ATS girls coincided with the twenty-first birthday party of one of them, to which Fan and Leonora were also invited. It must have been pretty hectic: forty girls to a thousand lonely officers! But for

Fan it turned out to be a very significant moment. She had already briefly met the handsome young Colonel John ('Jof') Hewlett, the artillery officer who was CO of the 58th Anti-Aircraft unit near to the orange grove villa on her arrival in Italy, without being unduly impressed. It seems he took the chance meeting much more seriously than Fan. since he volunteered to take Fan and Leonora to the party at Caserta in his staff car. The question then arose of whether the two girls dare attend the party out of uniform, which was officially not allowed. They had managed to bring with them a skirt, blouse and a pair of shoes each, and decided to break the rules for once, there being no FANY dragon around to discipline them. The girls had decided that Hewlett was 'rather boring', and they were determined to get rid of him so they could enjoy themselves. But how were they to get back to Naples? Fan did manage to lose him, but not before making sure their lift back was secured over drinks on the balcony, which enabled them to get to know each other.

It was hardly surprising that Hewlett came across as boring. The poor man's wife had died the day before he was posted overseas, leaving him a grieving widower with a baby son. His rather stilted approach to Fan is hardly surprising in the circumstances, and as we shall see subsequent meetings made a better impression on her.

Dodds-Parker was recalled to London to take part in the planning for D-Day and Fan found herself with a new boss. Major-General Stawell was a typical starchy old-style regular soldier. This did not fit well with the easy-going and informal ethos of the SOE, whose senior officers for whom Fan had worked, Gubbins, Dodds-Parker and Holdsworth had all impressed her with their intelligence and dedication, and they had all become good personal friends. This could not be said of Stawell at this point, although they met socially and on good terms after the war.

Stawell's ADC was a major from a combat unit who was anxious to return to his regiment in the front line, which he did. Fan now found herself promoted from ensign to captain in terms of the FANYs' rather idiosyncratic ranking system (the equivalent of major in Army ranking). She now found herself to the best of her knowledge the first female officer to be ADC to a general in an active theatre of war. It was to be a bumpy ride in all sorts of ways.

As always in Fan's war everything from tragedy to farce were to figure in her experience.

Much of Fan's work during this first period in Italy involved regular trips across to the Bari-Brindisi, on the east coast. It was here that agents were trained and dispatched on missions in Italy and the Balkan regions.

The winter of 1943/4 was exceptionally bad, and is remembered by FANY Rosemary Dacre, a wireless operator at Bari, for its exceptional cold, the only heating being a bowl of lighted charcoal placed under the table as a foot-warmer. Army rations were basic, and utterly incomprehensible to the locals who were employed as cooks. She recalls with horror a dish of porridge and bacon cooked together.

Throughout the summer of 1944 FANY wireless operators and coders worked flat out, as did Fan, who had had to cope alone with all General Stawell's coding and messages, as well as liaison visits to AFHQ and across to Bari, managing the general's diary, arrangements, domestic organisation, and providing accommodation and hospitality for visiting officers in transit.

FANY Milborough Walker (Lobanov Rostovsky) recalls this period when they were 'inundated with work': 'You might be at death's door, but you still went back to work when there was desperate need, and on occasions, when there was no room at a table, one would sit on the floor. Everything depended on getting a message right; speed and accuracy were all important, particularly the latter, and you just never had to lose your nerve.'

There were breaks from this frantic activity. Colonel 'Jof' Hewlett turned up again with an invitation for Fan to partner him at a dinner in the senior officers' mess in Naples. This she enjoyed, but was unable to repeat because there was a strict rule forbidding the fraternisation of male and female officers. She didn't see Hewlett again for some months.

At this time Stawell received a visitor. Baron Albert de Schonen, destined for a career in French national administration, had found himself called up for military service at the outset of war. At the defence of Sedan he won the *Croix de Guerre* for gallantry, but was taken prisoner. He escaped and was twice recaptured before being released in 1941 because of ill health. His attempt to cross the

Pyrenees to escape to Britain was almost frustrated by recapture, but using his alias as a wool buyer he got through and reached England via Portugal. He was recruited by SOE and was parachuted into the Cotes du Nord in early August 1944 with the 'Daniel' team, to provide arms for the resistance fighters. Recalled to England, he was sent on another mission in the Vosges, which failed in a German ambush. He was wounded, but rescued a comrade and drove him to a US Seventh Army field hospital advancing from the Mediterranean coast. He recovered from his wounds in an American military hospital in Naples, which is probably how he came to visit Stawell. He returned to England and continued to work as an instructor for volunteer French resistance fighters. He joined the French Diplomatic Service after the war and was subsequently advanced from officer to commander of the *Légion d'Honneur*.

Baron de Schonen offered his villa on the Amalfi coast near Ravello to Stawell for a break. Stawell accepted. Military regulations required Fan, as ADC, to be with the general at all times, but Stawell told her she was not to travel with him; that he had arranged for Colonel Hewlitt to drive her down to Amalfi separately. His reason for this was that Fan had to wait for an urgent message to be decoded and brought to him at Amalfi. On arrival they saw nothing of Stawell during the visit.

Fan's relationship with 'Jof' Hewlett really starts here, but she did not see him again until her return to London some time later. In the meantime more adventures were to come.

CHAPTER 14

An Egyptian Interlude: Fan sees Action

'Three poets, in distant ages born,
Greece, Italy, and England did adorn.
The first in loftiness of thought surpassed,
The next in majesty, in both the last.
The force of nature could no farther go;
To make a third she joined the other two.'
John Dryden

This is not the place for detailed discussion of the political complexities that in early 1944 bedevilled the arrangements for the transfer of control of SOE operations in the Mediterranean theatre from Cairo to Italy. The questions which had arisen revolved around the fact that resistance activities in the Balkans were conducted by two incompatible partisan forces, the basically communist partisans led by Tito and their deadly rivals, royalist partisans led by Mihaillovic, who were as inclined to fight each other over post-war supremacy as to fight the German occupying force.

There were also difficulties in reconciling the objectives and style of US and British military commands. After complex negotiations, in which Gubbins was involved, it was agreed that there should be created a section of AFHQ to control and direct special operations in Italy.

The technical problems involved in changing the wireless systems meant that communications with agents in the field in the Balkans continued to be centred on the SOE offices in Rustum buildings in Cairo for the time being. The military importance of SOE operations in the Balkans and Greece lay in the need to deceive the Germans into expecting and preparing to oppose a major assault via Greece. This would, like Operation Shingle (the Italian campaign), draw German reserves away from France, making the success of Operation Overlord (the D-Day landings) more likely.

Major-General Stawell had spent a period in command of SOE in Cairo, despite his service having being previously entirely within a regular army environment. This may explain Fan's lack of enthusiasm for either his style of command or his knowledge of special operations. It was from Cairo that he was moved to Naples to SOE (M) liaison HQ in place of Dodds-Parker.

Fan felt herself to be under a great deal of pressure, learning on the job the functions of ADC to a senior general, especially one so different from Gubbins, Dodds-Parker and Holdsworth. However, she continued to enjoy meeting a great variety of senior allied officers, as well as a great many fascinating characters who were working as agents in the field. She was, however, very much detached by distance and rank from the large numbers of FANYs working at Mola di Bari and back at Cairo and Algiers, never mind London. This meant that she missed much of the girlish camaraderie of the mostly younger women who had joined the FANY after her, including many in the Cairo station who were originally in the WAAF or other women's services but were transferred to FANY service after the usual interview with the fierce Gamwell and the usual training, conducted in Cairo.

By mid-1944 Cairo had been relieved of much of its work. Greece was about to fall to the Allies and the D-Day landings were under way. It must have been at about this point that Fan was instructed to accompany Stawell to Cairo, presumably to continue the wind-down process with Bickham Sweet-Escott and Brigadier Benfield. For Fan this was an exciting prospect, since her travel experience outside Britain was limited to Massingham in Algiers, and Naples and southern Italy.

Margaret Pawley (née Herbertson) paints a vivid picture of the life of a FANY in Cairo, where she served for some time. The first group of FANYs arrived in Cairo in December 1943, twenty coders under the command of Captain Norah Coggin. Tall, slim and elegant, always with hair in a French pleat and full dress uniform, Coggin was a stickler for smart appearance. Living quarters were assigned in a mansion in the suburb of Heliopolis, 7 miles from Cairo. From here they were transported by 3 ton trucks to the offices at Rustum Buildings in central Cairo. The offices suffered from unpleasant smells and the girls hung scented plants at the windows.

Coggins took great care to keep her girls in good health, seeking to avoid outbreaks of dysentery by insisting that only a handful of cleaner restaurants were to be used, and sugary groppy cakes (a great favourite after years of rationing) were restricted to one a day for the first three weeks. Despite the hectic shift work social life was not neglected entirely, especially at Christmas, when parties and dancing, and even turkey and plum pudding, were enjoyed. Gubbins and Dodds-Parker enjoyed dinner in the FANY mess very soon after the FANY contingent arrived.

Rare spells of leave allowed Pawley and other colleagues to do some sightseeing both in Egypt and even Palestine and Jerusalem. But life was not all fun and games. An outbreak of smallpox led to the death of a nineteen-year-old FANY, Jan Smith, despite the best efforts of an RMC officer who conducted a rather primitive mass vaccination.

For the first few months of her service in Cairo Pawley had been one of the WAAFs drafted in and later transferred to the FANY. During this period, before she moved to Heliopolis and the FANY mess, she lived on a houseboat on the Nile with colleagues.

Fan and General Stawell flew to Cairo from Brindisi via Malta, without incident. No one seemed to know what to do with a female ADC to a general, so she was allocated to the houseboat, now vacated by Pawley and her friends, where she found herself alone apart from a local servant. Very soon she found her watch had been stolen, and she felt very vulnerable. She was transported daily to Rustum Buildings by car driven by a major, but once there did not seem to have much to do. I suspect Stawell found it a little disconcerting to have a female ADC with the effective rank of major: it would have been outside his experience as a long-serving regular officer. He seems to have shared fewer confidences with Fan than Gubbins and Dodds-Parker had; he expected her merely to dance attendance on him.

Stawell did, however, take Fan on a day out to see the pyramids and the sphinx, with the two of them and Stawell's batman driver on camels. They returned safely, unlike the sergeant-major who was accompanying a group of adventurous FANYs on the same trip. The girls decided to climb to the top of the Great Pyramid accompanied by him, and he slipped while helping a FANY down a tricky stretch. She tried to prevent his fall, but could not carry his weight. He was killed instantly.

Fortunately Fan had a rather better experience. A passing Bedouin told her fortune, telling her that she had been married and would marry again at the end of the war, in the meantime returning to London. He was right.

The return journey to Italy brought more excitement. It was in a borrowed aircraft with a Greek pilot, stopping over at Athens, only liberated days before by British troops. Since the journey involved flying over Crete, which was still occupied by a German garrison, the pilot fortified himself with a few drinks. He was, according to Fan, drunk and terrified for the whole journey. Stawell constantly cursed and shouted at him to concentrate. As it happens he had good reason to be terrified, as Fan describes the puffs of black smoke as they were bombarded by anti-aircraft fire over Crete. The pilot obviously felt that his longed-for reunion with his wife was not going to happen.

They were to proceed in Athens to the Hotel Grand Bretagne; which had to be searched for booby traps before they could enter: the Germans had an unpleasant habit of fixing explosive devices to the underside of toilet seats.

The purpose of Stawell's visit was to congratulate the partisan leaders and thank them for their help in making the invasion a success. A grand dinner was arranged for these leaders, Stawell and a few British officers who had remained behind. Fan was the only woman present. From their gardens the locals had dug up many bottles of champagne and ouzo, hidden from the occupying Germans. The table was laid with the finest linen and dinner service, vast quantities of champagne were drunk – but dinner consisted of one Army issue hard biscuit each; Fan called them dog biscuits. The retreating Germans had denuded the city of every scrap of food, leaving the locals to starve.

Next day Fan was given the day off, and went out into the city in uniform: Suddenly she was more frightened than she had been on the plane. The entire population of Athens was delighted to see a British officer, and a woman at that, walking in Parliament Square after years of German occupation. She was mobbed by excited Greeks who wanted to hug her, and in doing so threatened to trample her to death. She ran like a hare back to the safety of the hotel.

The stay lasted two or three nights before they continued their journey, returning to Naples airport.

CHAPTER 15

The Fortunes of War

'We do not want Germans or Americans.
Let us weep in peace.'
Graffiti on a wall in Trastevere, Rome, January
1944

B itter fighting continued only a few miles to the north of the Naples villa. The seaborne landings at Anzio by the Fifth Army under the American General Clark took place on 22 January 1944, while the Eighth Army continued to push north towards Cassino on the Naples to Rome road. Both sides were aware of the significance of this advance up the spine of Italy. Even more so was it clear that the Anzio landings on the western coast of Italy would, if successful, lead to the link-up of the Fifth and Eighth Armies in an assault on Rome, and the rolling up of the Germans across Northern Italy. Attempts to prevent this would seriously weaken German defences in the face of the expected invasion in northern and southern France. Moreover, the symbolism of the reconquest of Rome was enormous: in 1907 G.M. Trevelyan, the historian of nineteenth-century Europe, had called Rome 'The living chronicle of man's long march to civilization'. Hitler too was well aware of the military and symbolic importance of Rome. His order of the day was described by a senior Wehrmacht officer as being like 'The call of a revolutionary fanatic'. Defeat at the Anzio beachhead would open up Route 7, the motorway connecting Rome with Naples to the west. Defeat at the other key German stronghold, Cassino, would open up Route 6, the central route from Rome to Naples. Anzio, to the south-west of Cassino, was first priority, and has been described since as 'the start of the invasion of Europe'. Hitler ordered reinforcements to move south, stressing the importance of Anzio; he ordered that 'every soldier must be aware of the importance of this battle', which was to be fought with 'holy hatred against the enemy who wages a ruthless war of annihilation against the German people'.

Setbacks at Anzio, and the stalemate at the town of Cassino and the great monastery of Monte Cassino, meant that the two armies did not link up until 25 May 1944.

During this period, while Fan was visiting Massingham on 6 February 1944, Michael Gubbins (son of General Gubbins) and Malcolm Munthe were escorting an Italian SOE courier, who was heading for Rome, across exposed no man's land. When they were raked by machine gun fire they had to leap into a trench. Munthe was seriously wounded, and Michael Gubbins was killed. Fan was with General Gubbins at Massingham when he received news of Michael's death, and walked with him for ages on the beach, consoling him as well as she could. By now Gubbins was Fan's close friend.

General Mark Clark, commanding the Fifth Army at Anzio, wrote in his diary that he and his opponent Vietinghoff, were like two boxers in a ring. 'I have committed my last reserve, and I am sure the Bosche [the Germans] have done the same.' Stalemate ensued in February, although there were times when the frenzied German efforts to drive back the Allied Fifth Army into the sea were close to succeeding. Meanwhile, in Rome itself, the occupying German forces behaved with great brutality towards the civilian former allies, aided by Fascist collaborators. Many young Roman men were rounded up for forced labour, and many lost their lives to Allied strafing from the air while they worked to keep the roads open.

The hold-up of the Allied advance caused the inhabitants of Rome to despair, and even resentment – hence the graffiti quoted at the start of this chapter. There appeared to be a strong likelihood that the Germans would be driven out of Rome only after complete destruction of the 'Eternal City'.

At the ancient strategic fortress city Cassino, in the mountains, conditions in January 1944 were worse than near the coast at Anzio, but the Germans had had time to construct a strong defensive position with concrete bunkers and gun emplacements built into the hillsides and even in the monastery of Monte Cassino itself, which stood on a hill north of the town. Cassino had been bombarded by the Allies in September 1943, and on 15 February 1944 it was pounded again by Allied bombers and the monastery destroyed, bringing 'the end of fourteen hundred years of tradition, devotion, art, and learning'. The Roman-Catholic world was outraged, handing a propaganda triumph to the Germans, who claimed correctly that many of the treasures at the monastery had been removed to safety, but wrongly (according to the Allies) that the monastery contained no German troops. Fortunately, by 1964 it had been completely rebuilt.

Bombs also fell on the outskirts of Rome. The pope made a public appeal to the 'vision and wisdom' of both sides to save the city from ruin. Meanwhile Rome starved as retreating German troops flooded the city, and there was bombing on 14 March.

The brutal fighting in front of Cassino in filthy winter weather was perhaps inevitable, and the destruction of the monastery was more than justified in the eyes of 90 per cent of the Allied troops, who saw it used as an observation post that directed the guns around the town that fired on the exposed Allied advance.Both sides were castigated for the disastrous bombing of Cassino, but many well-informed observers could not see how the Germans could have avoided defending this key point on the road to Rome in a valley only 6km wide, or the Allies could have avoided using any means to break through. General Clark himself described the fighting as 'The most gruelling, the most harassing, and in one respect the most tragic phase of the war in Italy'. Even more potential disasters to European culture lay ahead, on the road to Rome, Assisi, Sienna, Florence, Padua, Perugia, Pisa, Ravenna, Venice.

News and rumours about Cassino, and the possible defeat of the Allies at the Anzio beachhead, percolated back to Naples. Fan was aware of the intense rivalry and even dislike between the American and British senior officers in the Fifth and Eighth Armies, and was also aware of the determination of the American generals, especially Clark, to reach Rome before the British.

Recognising that the Allied forces at Anzio were faced by overwhelming odds, Lucas decided on a final assault before being overwhelmed by the German advance that was in preparation. Fantastic courage by the British troops led to the collapse of the German front at a key point, known as Wigan Street. This was the turning point, when the beachhead was secured; but lacking sufficient forces to advance, the Allies had to settle for stalemate from late February.

Success at Cassino led to the breakout at Anzio, and Operation Panther began on 19 March 1944. When New Zealand troops entered Cassino they found a scene described by a NZ corporal as 'a vision of the end of the world, past description'. A German corps commander, Senger, wrote: 'What I saw and felt took me back twenty-eight years, when I experienced the same loneliness crossing the battlefield of the Somme.' The bloody assault on the monastery continued throughout March, ending during a blizzard at the end of the month. Both sides were exhausted, and General Alexander planned the next Allied offensive, Operation Diadem, for mid-May. Meanwhile on 28 March, as Cassino fell, Vesuvius erupted, subsiding on the 29th after a spectacular display of eruptions of flame and red-hot rock being flung 1000ft into the sky.

On 26 March 1944 a German communiqué affirmed Rome's status as an 'open city'; German military personnel were to be moved out. But Italian resistance fighters were warned that any action on their part would cause the Germans to bring the military back and prepare to defend the city, thus ensuring its destruction by the Allies.

Meanwhile the Allies regrouped and prepared for advance on Rome. Operation Overlord, D-Day, was scheduled for early June. Air attacks rained down on military targets such as marshalling yards and main roads, but care was taken to avoid bombing historic cities such as Sienna, which had no great military significance but great historical importance.

Rivalry between the Allied commanders continued. By 5 May it had been decided by Alexander that an advance should take place along Route 6 to cut off the retreating German Tenth Army. The American General Clark was tipped off that the timing was to be Alexander's – and he was furious, determined that his troops should be the first to enter Rome. He asked Alexander to issue orders only through him, not to a subordinate. Alexander backed down: 'Rome is yours, you take it. If you can't take it I will send the Eighth Army over to take it.'

The race for Rome was on and Clark, despite later claims, was not the first Allied general to enter Rome.

CHAPTER 16

Rome and the End Game

'So may a thousand actions, once afoot,
End in one purpose, and be all well borne
Without defeat. Therefore to France, my liege.'
William Shakespeare

The week of 18 to 25 May 1944 was a critical moment in the Italian campaign. The Polish units captured Monte Cassino while the US II Corps took Formia. On the 23rd VII Corps broke out of the Anzio beachhead and Canadian troops pierced the Hitler line, and on the 25th Cisterna fell and the forces from the Anzio beachhead finally linked up with US II Corps. On 28 May the Germans withdrew from Aprilia, enabling the Fifth Army to advance on Rome, which they entered on 4 June. Two days later Allied forces embarked on the D-Day landings in Normandy. The German retreat in Italy gathered pace. The final bloody chapter of the war had begun in Normandy and the south of France, while the Russians entered southern Poland.

Meanwhile Fan was back in Naples with General Stawell. At the time she was unaware that all was not well with SOE (M). All she knew was that she had not developed the strong personal loyalty to her new boss that she had felt for Gubbins and Gerry Holdsworth, both of whom led from the front, had a strong intellectual grasp of what SOE was about and were highly effective leaders. Fan felt that Stawell lacked these characteristics. His rigid regimental 'stiffness' alienated those he led, while she felt that his style made it difficult for him to cope with the complex and fast-moving world of special operations. It was not to be long before their mutual antipathy was to come to a climax.

For some time Gubbins had been developing serious reservations about Stawell's ability to handle the increasingly acrimonious relationships that had developed over the role of SOE (M) as the Italian campaign climaxed and the Germans retreated in Italy and the Balkans. Attention was focusing increasingly on the Western Front. The establishment of HQ BAF under Air Vice-Marshal Elliot brought matters to a head in May 1944. This was to control the supply of very limited air transport resources for SO (M), and conflicts of interest arose between BAF, whose sphere of interest was the entire Mediterranean, and SO (M), whose sphere was Northern Italy and the Balkans. Stawell was no match for the forceful Elliot, despite Gubbins having made what he felt were satisfactory arrangements with General Gammell, SACMED (Senior Allied Commander Mediterranean) Chief of Staff, about special operations in the area. The problems were compounded by the decision to prune clandestine activities in 'country' sections in favour of paramilitary activities. Gubbins was infuriated by what he saw as Stawell's passivity in the face of pressure from BAF for SO (M) to become, as Gubbins put it, a 'Harrods,' responsible for little more than the logistics of supply. In a coldly angry message to Stawell, he wrote: 'To what level have we sunk! In the present situation we seem to have got to the point where RAF are pinching everything for their territory, whereas in truth Italian Resistance (supported by SO (M)), is paying a far better and more immediate dividend. The war is drawing to a close and Germany is breaking up. I want you now to concentrate on the next moves which I hope will be Austria, Hungary, and NE Italy, which is the crucial point in your theatre.'

Clearly Stawell was living on borrowed time. Fan is unclear about exact timings of events at the beginning of June 1944, but it must have been on or about the 1st when Stawell ordered her to make arrangements for them to leave Naples and head north to Sienna, and then to Rome. He was to meet a very important Italian resistance agent probably at Sienna, which was to be a SO (M) forward station during the next few months.

The journey north was Fan's first real taste of frontline warfare. Cassino and its great monastery had been taken by the Allies only hours earlier. Not a single building in the city had survived the Allied bombing raids and artillery fire intact. The civilian population had for the most part moved out during the prolonged battle and was now straggling back. The roads were clogged with military conveys, the area was still heavily mined up to the verges, and thousands of corpses lay where they had fallen. Fan still shudders at the thought of the smell.

They entered Rome close on the heels of the retreating German forces, so close that if Fan is right they were actually in Rome before the advancing US units of the Fifth Army. It is ironic that Stawell, out of favour with Gubbins, should never have had the credit he perhaps deserved for being the first senior officer from the Allied armies to enter Rome.

Fan's SOE career almost came to an untimely end at this point in an incident that provides our only authentication for her claim to be first to Rome. On their last night before retreating, German senior officers held a leaving party in the palazzo that had been commandeered for their use. To it they invited all the contessas and high-class ladies of the city for a final night of debauchery. As the Yanks entered the city just a few hours later a liberation party was organised in the palazzo for senior Allied officers. Naturally the ladies who had entertained the Germans the night before returned in force. Fan was instructed to accompany Stawell to the celebration, driven by his Cockney batman. As ADC to a major-general, she was required to accompany Stawell everywhere, and this rather cramped his style. As we saw earlier, when visiting the Amalfi villa he had often disappeared – but Fan's delight at a few hours' freedom turned to serious concern when she saw her general disappearing up the staircase with a very beautiful contessa on his arm. Her concern was not for his moral welfare but for the time: it was near to midnight, and she was responsible for returning him in one piece to their billet through a chaotic and dangerous city. Her concern became close to panic as the clock ticked on towards morning, with no sign of the general. She had had the presence of mind to notice which bedroom he had entered, but did not relish the idea of disturbing him. When everyone else had left, however, she had no alternative. First, she beseeched the Cockney private who was their driver to knock on the door and remind the gallant general of his duty – but she received a dusty answer. 'Not bleeding likely! It's more than my life's worth!' 'Nothing else for it then,' thought Fan, and she marched up the fine staircase, with her driver, and tentatively approached Stawell's door. Not a sound was to be heard. A gentle knock produced no response, so Fan plucked up all her courage, knocked loudly, opened the door and marched in, eyes averted, and saluted smartly. 'Sir, it's 2am and the driver's worried about our safety. We really should go.' She did a smart salute and about-turn, and marched out, eyes still averted, followed by a string of curses from a very angry general.

An angry silence prevailed on the short journey, and Fan expected the worst next day. The next morning she was confronted by a still-furious general. 'I'm sending you back to London immediately!' was his brisk opening. Fan drew herself up to her full 5ft, looked Stawell in the eye, smiled ever so slightly and replied, 'On what charges?' The general thought for a moment, grunted and broke eye contact. Nothing more was said.

Shortly afterwards Fan and the general were driven back to Naples, where they remained for the rest of the summer and autumn of 1944.

Margaret Pawley, of Peter Lee's security section, arrived in Rome on 11 June, some six days after the departure of the Germans and Fan's misadventures, believing herself to be the first FANY to Rome. Her comments on the journey north match those made by Fan. She too was horrified by Cassino, and she vividly describes the privations faced by the small team of FANYs in Rome. They were accommodated first in the basement of the villa that belonged to a ninety-year-old contessa, whose resident nun-nurses left little for the FANYs to eat from the army rations which were the price of their accommodation. They moved from there to another dark and dingy basement, then to the turrets of a building on the outskirts of Rome. The theft of the Fiat on which they relied for transport precipitated another move to a flat nearer to their office. Gerry Holdsworth, always eager to be near the front line, arrived from Monopoli in early autumn with his FANY PA Gundred Grogan, and among others, Rosemary Dawe, a FANY wireless operator, whose description of life in Rome that year is recorded by Margaret Pawley: 'We slept in an icy flat, trudging in the snow up and down the Via Paroli. I sometimes slept in all my clothes, including my greatcoat.' Another FANY, Patricia Wilson, wrote to her parents on 29 January 1945: 'The billet we now have is a hotel. It is definitely the best FANY billet I have ever had, but cruelly cold, you probably have some idea how cold it is here, but it is colder than that!' Despite the cold and other privations, several FANYs met and courted their future husbands at this time.

Meanwhile the onset of the harsh winter brought the Italian campaign to a standstill at the German defensive position, the Gothic Line, which stretched across Northern Italy just south of Bologna. Field Marshal Alexander, the Allied Supreme Commander in Italy, had lost six divisions to the campaign in France, while heavy snow hampered operations. There was no further movement until the spring of 1945. The frontline troops suffered terribly in the constant snow and rain from influenza and dysentery. With stalemate on the frontline, the Germans concentrated on a brutal sweep over the countryside, killing partisans and peasants indiscriminately.

Soon after the fall of Rome Stawell fell ill and was repatriated to England. Fan was also ordered to return to London and to report to 64 Baker Street for orders. At the beginning of the new year Stawell was still in hospital and unlikely to return to duty. Fan was more anxious than ever about her future, but a new chapter was about to begin.

CHAPTER 17
Choices, Choices!

'Till looking on an Englishman, the fairest that
eye could see,
Her fancy fell a-turning ...'
William Shakespeare

In the Knightsbridge flat, after a lonely Christmas, Fan was
disorientated and anxious. Her life had been taken over since
1941 by the SOE. She had no home, no certainty of continued
employment as a FANY and no other job to go to. Apart from
her keep and the minuscule war office allowance (originally 2s 6d
per week and not much more now), she had little income. She had
had no home leave since going to Algeria, and had lived in uniform
for four years.

Despite the bomb damage, London in 1945 must have seemed
surprisingly normal after the horrors of Cassino and the privations
of Rome. The war in Europe was clearly nearing its end, although
there was the ever-present and entirely random threat of the V1
buzz bombs, and then the silent and deadly V2 rockets.

To her delight and relief Fan received a message from General
Gubbins early in the New Year, instructing her to report to 64 Baker
Street: he had a job for her. In her first spell at Baker Street she had,

like most of her contemporaries, developed tremendous respect and affection for this dynamic and charismatic officer. There was no suggestion of a romantic liaison; her affection for Gubbins was more that for a close friend. Imagine her delight on being reunited with her hero, and her embarrassment when he greeted her with, 'I hear you did a grand job in the Med!' Margaret Jackson, his personal assistant throughout the war, had resigned, worn out with the strain. He wanted Fan, his other much-trusted FANY officer, to take over. 'Do you think you can bear me after all the excitement?' he said. In any other context he would have been on the receiving end of a giant hug, but the proprieties of military life prevailed.

Bickham Sweet-Escott, whom Fan had met during her time in the Mediterranean theatre, also reported back to Baker Street at this time, aware that in Southern and Central Europe there was really nothing more for SOE to do. Like Fan he thought of finding a posting outside SOE, but was persuaded that the war in the Far East with Japan was likely to last another two or two and a half years. He accepted a posting there in January 1945, having been told that jobs in that theatre carried a rank at least one pip higher than anywhere else; this meant he would make full colonel. Meanwhile Force 133, the Mediterranean branch of SOE, was being disbanded.

Force 136 (South East Asia) had an even more complex structure and management arrangement than the quite sufficiently confused Force 133. Gubbins had much to do managing these operations, while simultaneously fighting off the strong pressures for the total disbanding of SOE. Gubbins reported to his political boss, Lord Selbourne, that Britain should not be the only Great Power left without such a facility after the war. These political machinations kept Fan very busy.

By the time the Nazi Reich finally collapsed, as the Russian forces entered Berlin in May 1945, and the war in Europe came to an end, the war in South East Asia seemed far from over. Gubbins was struggling, unhappily, to accept that in this theatre of war SOE had to play second fiddle to their American equivalent, OSS – which had an ulterior motive: building a position in which American policy could be furthered in a post-war world. This had become clear to Gubbins during his visit to Washington in autumn 1944.

Force 136 was as taken by surprise as almost everybody else when America dropped an atom bomb on Hiroshima in July 1945, precipitating the surrender of Japan. Fan's military career was almost over.

Comedy was never far away for Fan. After a particularly hard day at 64 Baker Street in spring 1945, Gubbins invited her to join him for dinner. They took off in a staff car to Knightsbridge, where they parked before crossing the road to the Knightsbridge Grill. This could have been Fan's most embarrassing moment! A word of explanation is needed here. Like all the women's uniformed services (only more so), FANY officers were required to observe a very strict dress code, especially when serving in a unit commanded by a senior 'dragon'. Uniform was to be worn at all times, on or off duty, except on very rare social occasions. This included the particularly irksome Army issue khaki woollen knickers, with legs. Those like Fan who were serving in solo roles in a largely male unit were inclined to disobey this particular order. By now, after five years' service, Fan had very little in the way of a civilian wardrobe, but she had made sure that she had less unpleasant underwear. It was a matter of morale! As she crossed busy Knightsbridge High Street at 10pm the elastic of her silk knickers snapped, and they dropped to the ground. Fan's embarrassment can only be imagined. Gubbins responded as an officer and a gentleman, suggesting that she step out of them. He quickly picked them up and said, 'Come on, let's go and eat,' and led her across the road. Nothing more was said until the end of the meal, when he slipped the offending garment surreptitiously into her hand, suggesting that she retire to the ladies' room to effect running repairs. This display of gallantry and presence of mind goes some way to explain her affection for this 'perfect gentleman'.

As the war ground to a halt Fan received an invitation to dinner from a surprising quarter. Lt-Col. John Oliver Frederick Hewlett RA had met Fan back in 1943 in Naples when he was CO of the anti-aircraft unit from which Fan had scrounged rations. They had met again when he had taken her to a dance. Fan had not thought much more of him for two years, but he had obviously never forgotten her. 'Jof' Hewlett had endured a tragic war. His young wife having died the day before he went overseas with his regiment, he did not see his tiny son for the next six years. When he returned, his son had been effectively abducted (as Fan saw it) by Jof's three sisters, whom Fan found to be very unpleasant. They were so unkind to her that to this day she refers to them as the three witches.

To Fan's complete astonishment, the dinner ended with an unexpected declaration of love and a proposal of marriage. She was taken aback. Only days before Gubbins had given her a post-war job, which she was reluctant to refuse. He was to go on a world trip, to visit OSS in Washington and SOE stations in Canada and South East Asia, and he was eager for her to accompany him. Fan was in a turmoil. What should she do? The prospect of a world trip was very enticing, but on the other hand what would she do when she came back? The war was over; she had no job, no home and little money.

Jof's caring manner made a much better impression this time round, and the next day Fan told Gubbins of the offer. He swore, as he would be left in the lurch for his trip, and arranged to take Fan and Hewlett to dinner at the Knightsbridge Grill. There Jof apologised, they shook hands and Gubbins sighed, 'You win!' Having been successfully persuaded that Jof's intentions were entirely honourable, and that Fan would be in safe hands, he gave the match his blessing and advised Fan to go ahead.

A little later Gubbins called Fan into his office and sat her down. On the table were rows of medals. 'I think you've earned a reward for your service. Which do you think you'd like?' Fan was taken aback: the thought of a 'gong' had never occurred to her. She thought of the FANYs who had served behind enemy lines with such courage, and of the many who had lost their lives in horrific circumstances. 'No, I don't think I deserve a medal.' 'As you wish,' said Gubbins.

When Fan accepted Jof Hewlett's offer of marriage a new and surprising chapter opened. Being a born southerner, Fan had doubts: did she really want to go and live in Hartlepool, where Jof was finance director of Cameron's Brewery? But she said yes anyway.

CHAPTER 18

Marriage and the North Country

'My desolation does begin to make
A better life.'
William Shakespeare

F an had not been fazed by her hectic and adventurous
wartime exploits in Algeria, Egypt, Greece and Italy, but
did find the prospect of a new life in the even more alien
surroundings of a northern industrial town rather
forbidding.

There was no time for the usual prolonged period of preparation, choosing venue, reception, guest list, bridesmaids, best man and, most important, the wedding dress. Choosing what to wear was no problem for a serving officer, as best mess dress is impressive on a handsome young man at his wedding, but Fan's choice was more difficult. She had worn FANY uniform almost exclusively for five years and had no up-to-date wardrobe. She was intensely proud of her war service in the FANY (she has remained a member of the Special Forces Club throughout her life), but to be married in uniform was not an option: Jof was determined that she should have a special dress. In 1945 finding something suitable was difficult, but eventually Fan gave in gracefully and accepted a badly fitting suit purchased from Harrod's, which she so disliked that she has nothing to say about it.

The wedding took place on 23 September 1945 at St Stephen's, Victoria, the parish church of a FANY friend. Jof's second in command was best man. Only Fan's sister and her husband represented her family, but she was much cheered by the presence of her friend, mentor and boss Major-General Colin Gubbins, who gave her away in the place of her father. General Stawell and Amy, his wife, also came to the wedding. Fan had met Jof's family when they made the trip to Harrogate to have lunch with them. This was rather spoilt by Jof's sister, who remarked that she knew of the FANYs: 'camp followers!' Both Jof and Fan had resigned their commissions, and after a brief honeymoon they drove north to start a new life in Hartlepool.

Here Fan suddenly and disconcertingly found herself mistress of a huge Victorian house, the Hewlett family home before the war and part of Cameron's Brewery's property estate; it was located next to the brewery on the outskirts of Hartlepool. Jof's father, a partner in the brewery, had previously lived there, and Fan recalls it as 'full of cobwebs and cold'. Moving in was a nightmare. In an example of the culture clash that occurred, Jof's mother went to the grocer's in a horse and carriage, remaining there with a rug over her knees while the grocer did the shopping for her. The grocer was horrified when Fan walked in to do her own shopping.

This gritty Geordie town depended on heavy industry: coal, steel, shipbuilding. The war had brought a degree of prosperity to an area that had been brought to its knees by the unemployment and poverty of the Great Depression of the 1930s, but times were hard everywhere. Rationing of food and petrol was to continue for several more years. Everything was scarce, but it was probably a profitable time for the brewery.

Up to this point Fan had had neither inclination nor opportunity to play the dutiful housewife. No doubt she tackled the task with all the administrative skill, tact and diplomacy that she demonstrated in her FANY career, when, as Gubbins put it when she became

General Stawell's aide, she was the 'most efficient FANY in the Mediterranean'. In that role she was used to dealing with a variety of very senior British and American officers and politicians, not to mention volatile and highly stressed SOE agents of all nationalities. Now she had to be equally solicitous to seriously boring local worthies.

Hartlepool's borough council was completely Labour dominated after the landslide victory by Attlee in the 1945 General Election, but Jof was somehow elected in the council elections of 1946 as the only Conservative councillor. He seems to have won the respect and affection of the Labour councillors, who in 1951 invited him to become Lord Mayor. This threw Fan into a round of civic activities in support of her husband as Lady Mayoress. The endless round of civic engagements in a provincial English town must have seemed very tedious, but there were compensations. She was lucky enough to find a friend, a WAAF officer who was a wartime colleague.

In 1947 Fan and Jof's only son Nick was born; meanwhile Fan had had to overcome the difficulties of being stepmother to Jof's son Richard. By the time Fan was immersed in civic duties he was away at Oundle School.

The death of King George VI in 1952 and succession of the young Queen Elizabeth II brought with it the prospect of a coronation. It became clear that Hartlepool's Lord Mayor and Lady Mayoress would be invited to attend, as would others in their position nationwide. It is a great tribute to Jof's standing in the community that the Labour council decided to invite him to serve a second year as Lord Mayor. This was very unusual: the job was normally rotated around the parties represented on the council. It was obviously felt that a distinguished figure was needed to cope with the niceties of royal protocol. Fan has little to say about what must have been a busy and exciting time preparing for the big day in June 1953. We can only imagine the hustle and bustle of buying the correct attire.

The prospect of a few exciting days back in London must have brightened up a rather dull provincial life in those dreary post-war years. But as always there were compensations and hilarious moments. It made Fan very sad when civic dinners and other social events caused her to leave her little son in the care of Mary, their elderly housekeeper; she would have much preferred to read him a bedtime story. These civic events, though, were not without their funny side. On one occasion Fan found herself required to make a speech responding to the Lord Lieutenant of the county. She remembers taking the notes for her speech inside her glove. Once on her feet she removed the glove, only to discover that the early ballpoint pen she had used had (as they often did) leaked ink, ruining her glove and obliterating her notes. Overwhelmed with embarrassment, she held up her stained hands and said, 'I'm sorry, I can't remember what I was going to say.' After a brief silence an elderly lady spoke up: ' Never mind, love, you look lovely.' Fan's day was saved by a vigorous round of applause.

As Mayor, Jof was required to take his chain of office (miniature fishing boats of great value) to London for the Coronation. The Mayor had no expenses allowance, so Jof and Fan stayed in the Special Services Club. The macebearer could not stay there, so Fan and Jof had no choice but to take the chain with them to dinner, and sleep with it between them in their double bed. After the ceremony at Westminster Abbey they eventually found their way back to the club, together with regalia, which again spent the night in their bed for safety.

The day itself must have been rather less enjoyable than Fan expected. It was a dismal, dark and drizzly day, more like November than June. The wives of civic dignitaries from all round England found themselves corralled in the area around the fountain in the Mall opposite the entrance to Buckingham Palace. Here Fan and her stepson Richard were marooned for six hours or more; but of course they had a superb view of the royal procession leaving after the ceremony. Fan's recollection of the day is rather more prosaic, being very cold and desperate for the toilet!

During this period Fan did not entirely lose touch with General Stawell and General Gubbins. By 1945 Stawell's wife Amy had realised how well her husband had been looked after, especially when he fell ill and had to return to hospital in England. Her letter expressing her thanks was clearly written in some embarrassment, after her cold greeting when she met her husband and Fan off the train at Paddington. She was clearly grateful, and Jof and Fan visited the couple for a weekend soon after the end of the war. They were also guests at several weddings of former SOE colleagues, notably Malcolm Munthe.

Perhaps the couple's most enjoyable excursion was to retrace their steps in Southern Italy, where they first met. They revisited the villa at Orange Grove, Naples, and the SOE office at Moli de Bari, and were entertained for a few days in the beautiful villa, La Rondinala, which perches on a cliff high near Ravello on the Amalfi coast and is accessible only on foot. It was here that Fan had accompanied General Stawell and Jof back in 1943. The villa was owned by Baron Albert de Schonen, an SOE officer who was to distinguish himself during 1944 when he led a team of SOE agents, together with Capt. Ed Bennett and Sgt Ron Brierley, who were parachuted into Cotes du Nord. Their team, codenamed Daniel, provided arms for the resistance fighters who were hampering the German retreat. In their next operation, codenamed Gregory, in the Vosges region, Bennett and de Schonen were wounded, the latter dragging his wounded colleague to safety and driving him to a field hospital of the US Seventh Army which was advancing from the south. He later became a member of the French diplomatic service.

Only six months into Jof's second year as major, shortly after the Coronation in 1953, disaster was to take place. Fan's time in Hartlepool was drawing to a close. As so often seems to have happened in her life, a disaster was to be the precursor of another new challenge.

CHAPTER 19

Back to Square One

'Difficulties mastered are opportunities won.'
Winston Churchill

After the Coronation, Fan's even if dull provincial life continued. Richard was away at school, but she still had the household to run. This deceptive calm was not to last. Jof was a proud man, and he betrayed nothing of his worries about his business life, so it was a total shock when he came home one evening in a state of great distress. Fan comforted him as best she could. Finally, in tears, he said, 'I've done a terrible thing. We're jobless, homeless and without a car!' Increasingly concerned with the way company finances were being handled, as a matter of honour Jof had felt obliged to resign. The house belonged to the company, as did their car.

A frantic search began for new employment, and by great good fortune a similar post was found to be vacant at Hammonds Brewery in Bradford, West Yorkshire. So Fan found herself beating a hasty retreat from the land of impenetrable Geordie speech to the equally incomprehensible world of West Yorkshire.

While settling into his new job Jof stayed at the Alexandra Hotel in Bradford, and poor Fan found herself condemned to stay with the three sisters. After six weeks Jof picked Fan up on Sunday morning to drive to Bradford for lunch and house-hunting. It was a dismal foggy day, so they retreated to the nearby Branch Hotel. Jof asked the barmaid, 'Where are we?' 'Shipley,' was the reply. 'Do you know of a home for sale?' said Jof. The barmaid recommended 13 Victoria Park, a pleasant four-bedroom Victorian residence. They bought the house, despite it lacking a sunny aspect, and stayed there for three years. Meanwhile Jof came across an acquaintance from his Territorial Army days, whom he had last met at the TA Coronation dinner. He gave Jof and Fan an entry into Bradford's middle-class social scene.

One Bank Holiday Monday, in August 1956, Jof suggested they go house-hunting again. They fell in love with a large Victorian villa, standing on a hilltop in open country, about 4 miles from Bradford. Smithfield House, Allerton Road, had some Victorian eccentricities: a hotplate in the dining room, a kitchen hatch, a large barn and a garden toilet. The large garden included a fishpond, into which the brother of Nick's girlfriend was later to fall, squashing all the goldfish, during Nick's twenty-first birthday party. Fan remembers with delight the remains of an Adam fireplace that they scavenged from a tip at Six Days Only, a hamlet near the village of Idle on the outskirts of Bradford. Once she had removed the old layers of paint, very carefully with jewellers' tools, Greek figures and designs were revealed. She lovingly restored it and it was installed in the lounge. The task took her six months!

As it turned out the new house was ideal for the family's needs, and until they had a car again Hammonds Brewery could be easily reached, with a 3 mile ride by trolley bus followed by a short walk up Manchester Road. Domestic life at Smithfield House was much as before, but without domestic staff. Fan seems to have found Yorkshire folk rather more to her taste than the Geordies, and they soon acquired a circle of friends among the professional and business community in this tight-knit Yorkshire town.

Richard was now at Oundle School, while Nick started school at the local prep school, Rossfield, before going to Red House at Green Hammerton near York, then the Leys School at Cambridge.

In the late 1950s Bradford was still the centre of the West Yorkshire textile manufacturing district. Set in a basin surrounded by hills rising to 1300ft, with many miles of moorland stretching west towards Haworth, home of the Brontës, north towards upper Airedale and east towards the great bulk of Ilkley Moor and beautiful Wharfedale. The town itself was a collection of overgrown villages, with a centre containing a fine array of Victorian municipal buildings, the Wool Exchange, great Victorian warehouses in Little Germany, and the ancient parish church (now cathedral) of St. Peter. From the hills surrounding the city it looked like a pin cushion, with over 100 mill chimneys. Unfortunately these mills were still driven by great Victorian mill engines, and the railway traffic was still steam hauled: it was said, rightly, that you could only see from one side of the city to the other during one week of the year, Bowling Tide week, when the mills shut down for their annual holiday. The prevailing features in winter were rain, snow and dense fog.

This apparently grim environment was compensated for by a close-knit community life among these tough Yorkshire characters, although social class divided the community. John Braine's novel *Room at the Top* (1953) describes this alien world well. Insular though it was, the business community depended on exports – of spun yarn, wool tops and fine worsted cloth. The mill-owners were a well-travelled fraternity, and even the biggest bank, Barclays, had a full-scale branch office dealing only in foreign currency exchange for the export trade. This was situated only a few yards from the Wool Exchange, the centre of business life and gossip.

The social life of business and professional classes centred around the Masonic movement and the Bradford Club. The latter was entirely inaccessible to aspiring working-class grammar school boys. Other centres of social life, mainly but not exclusively for the womenfolk, were the two great department stores, Brown Muff's and Busby's, both now long gone. Apart from up-market shopping, the former boasted a coffee lounge on the top floor where woolmen did deals over morning coffee before or after 'going on' Change, next door. The coffee was good, the atmosphere that of the smoke room of a gentlemen's club, and all the daily papers were available.

By the end of the 1960's the city was unrecognisable. John Poulson, T. Dan Smith and their political sponsors had bulldozed much of the Victorian centre and replaced it with ugly concrete buildings, which in turn have been demolished in recent years.

Nevertheless Bradford still had, as it did pre-war, more millionaires than any comparable English city. By now serious money was gradually moving out of town to Wharfedale, Airedale and the outer suburbs. The age of car ownership changed everything. The old city became poorer as manufacturers struggled to survive, using a growing influx of cheap labour from Pakistan.

CHAPTER 20
Haute Couture

'My silks and fine array ...'
William Blake

Jof's oldest friend, Jim Gibb, was from his childhood in West Hartlepool, and it was he who played a part in starting Fan's new and exciting career in *haute couture*. Like Jof, Jim had trained as an accountant and was now managing director of an engineering firm in Manchester. Fan helped him find a flat in Manchester, and 'adopted' Jim's daughter, who was at boarding school in Harrogate. Sadly Jim and his wife had recently divorced, so when he fell ill as a consequence of the stress he had been under, Fan took him in at Smithfield House until he recovered. His convalescence was completed by a trip with Fan and Jof in his big Rover to Spain. In general the two men shared the driving, but Fan found herself taking the mountainous section from Perpignan to north-eastern Spain; while the men slept off the wine they had enjoyed at lunchtime.

When they returned Jim had fully recovered, to Fan's great relief. He and Jof went out to celebrate with plenty of champagne, rather inconsiderately leaving Fan at home. When they eventually arrived back Fan was not best pleased at the time or their condition, so she took no notice when Jof said, 'What does it feel like to be a lady of property?' Then the doorbell rang, and a man announced himself as Jerry Robinson of Dacre, Son and Hartley, the leading local estate agent. 'How does property weigh on your shoulders?' he said, once they had sat down with gin and tonics for all.

Robinson explained that Jof and Jim had invested in a unit in a small retail development that was being built 2 miles down Allerton Road towards Bradford. There were originally to be eight units, each with a flat above, but this had been reduced to four large units, of which Jof and Jim bought a middle one. The end unit next to it was taken by a greengrocer, who only lasted three weeks. The other end unit was to be a hardware store, and one of the middle units was to be a grocer's. 'What will you do with the shop, Fan? We can let the flat.' Fan responded rather indignantly that she knew nothing about shopkeeping and would have to think about it. Perhaps it was the result of spending five years of her younger life in a FANY uniform, with no chance to dress up, that influenced her decision. A little time later her mind was made up. Looking at a copy of *Vogue* lying on the coffee table, she said to Jim, '*Haute couture*. That's what I'll do.'

Next, Fan thought about how to fit out the shop. The owner of a major Bradford firm of plumbers' merchants, whose son was at prep school with Nic, offered carpet for the showrooms, left over from refurbishing their offices,. Now they needed a shopfitter. Fan went down the road to Allerton and called on the local undertaker: in those days 'joiner and undertaker' was how such tradesmen usually described themselves. 'No, I do coffins,' said Les. 'Why not diversify?' Few people could say no to Fan, so Les agreed to build whatever she wanted. 'We need lots of posh boxes and big double windows,' thought Fan. Drawings were done, carpets laid, fixtures fitted, and some pretty antique chairs, which had belonged to Jim's sister, completed the interior. Fan French-polished the fixtures herself.

What was she to sell? Where was the stock to come from? How was she to find customers? These were critical problems to a beginner. She decided only to target the middle-class ladies of the Bradford social circuit as customers, and that she would only sell formal and semi-formal ladies' wear from top designers, but which ones? Her initial choices included Frank Usher and Jean Veronner.

She wrote letters to all leading designers after a careful study of *Vogue* and *Harpers Bazaar,* the top fashion magazines of the time. As a result several of them were invited to display their samples at a viewing on the terrace at Smithfield House. Choices were made and the shop was stocked.

Opening day approached. On the penultimate night Jof and Jim decided to organise a party to 'wet the baby's head'. Caterers were brought in; lots of guests were invited. Jof turned up and, doing his best to help, fitted the models back to front, boobs at the back, after testing the champagne! At the party his leg was well pulled.

Next morning Fan was very busy dressing the window. Just as she finished a car drew up. In a panic Fan thought to herself, 'Shall I run out of the back door?' A lady entered and asked to try on several shirts. She bought two, and as she was the first customer Fan stuck her bill on the wall (£6 11s 6d), where it stayed for many years. The customer became a valued regular.

Fan's first marketing venture was a fashion show at Allerton Church Hall, the proceeds for charity, entry 2s 6d. She needed models, and after putting the word round she found eight girls, as well as an old gramophone to provide a musical background. It was a great success and the hall was full. The show was repeated at intervals at rather more up-market venues, such as the Bankfield Hotel, Bingley, and the Norfolk Gardens Hotel, Bradford. Fan's shows became a feature of the local social calendar. Her shop was well launched, and two reliable ladies were hired as staff, allowing Fan to go to trade shows.

Some time later, at the House of Frank Usher show in London, Fan was accompanied by Jim. One of the items shown was a full-length gold lamé gown for evening wear. Jim was very keen for Fan to buy it, and although she thought it 'extremely vulgar', and that it would lower the tone in her shop, she bought it anyway. It sold two hours after she put it on display! A lesson learned.

Two years went by and the shop was trading well. When the grocer next door failed Fan bought his premises, to create showrooms and a workroom. Later the remaining unit became available and Fan was able to extend her business further. Showrooms were extended and a large portion of the first floor, where the flats had been, were converted into workshops for alterations and bespoke work. A good staff was built up, and Fan was able to take off to the design fairs in Milan, Paris and so on, to choose the top garments.

By 1965 Nick had left the Leys with something of a reputation as a pianist. For a time he worked at Eddison's, an estate agent in Bradford. He wanted to join Fan in her business, but she felt that he needed retail training first. By chance, while on holiday, Fan met the training director of Harrods, and discussed the possibility of his company employing Nick – although both she and Jof had little confidence in his capacity for hard work; Jof actually wrote to Harrods to suggest that Nick might not be suitable. They took him on anyway, recognising his potential for their music department. Fan was able to recommend him for a share in a flat tenancy in the Special Forces Club. Nick was very successful at Harrods, but by 1969 had returned to Bradford to marry his fiancée Anna and to join Fan's business. He wanted to join his mum and build a chain of stores; he loved his occasional trips with her to the design fairs. Sara's (which was to have been Fan's daughter's name had her child been a girl) was now the name in women's high-class outfitting. Nick wanted a men's department, which he got, and to build a chain of stores, which they eventually did, under the name Hewlett's.

A reluctant Fan decided that Nick would have to prove his worth. She took him to several trade shows, starting with Frank Usher's. At each show Fan insisted on having two order forms, one for her and one for Nick: they were to watch the catwalk and jot down the items they thought they could sell. Fan was convinced that Nick would be much more interested in the content of the gowns than the gowns themselves; she was (at least partly!) wrong. To her astonishment he chose 90 per cent the same as she did – so she had no excuse to keep him out.

Nick took over the planned refurbishment of the premises, and in the following year's trade show at Munich was a great success again, both in his choice of stock and in his ability to charm the designers. He was a natural at the rag trade and inched his way into the business.

By 1970 the business was a great success, but it had taken its toll on Fan's health.

CHAPTER 21

Mothers and Sons

*'We are happier in many ways when we are
old than when we were young. The young sow
wild oats. The old grow sage.'*
Winston Churchill

F an would probably have been happy to run Sara's in
Allerton for the rest of her working life. The shop was
beautifully fitted out. She had five reliable staff on the sales
side, and five seamstresses in the workshop. Everybody
who was anybody in the West Riding came to Sara's for high-class
evening and day wear, and accessories. The men's department was
efficiently run by an old boy of Bradford Grammar School, Robin
Johnson. Her shop was profitable and fun to run.

Nick wanted more, though. In 1980, through an acquaintance,
Nick discovered an empty shop in Doncaster, which he insisted on
buying. Fan had already acquired outlets in Halifax and Wakefield,
which were good choices as there as still plenty of textile money in
Calderdale, Halifax and Huddersfield. The Doncaster shop was a
decent earner and Fan was happy with it, despite not having
wanted to expand; she had done her best to satisfy Nick's ambition.
Despite Fan's reservations, he had turned out to be a great success.

113

His management style was dynamic and strong, and he was good at dealing with staff and clients. The staff loved him, and his skill in buying the right stock ensured that the shops were a great success. Fan loved her son dearly, and her only unease was regarding his spending habits. He lived the lifestyle!

The partnership continued through the difficult years of the 1970s and 1980s Sara's continued to be a success, especially the original store, despite the economic crisis that had devastating effects on the local manufacturing industries, on textiles and engineering. The Doncaster store closed shortly after the miners' strike, and the closure of local pits and related industries left no disposable income for high fashion in the area.

Their dear friend and partner Jim Gibb worked with Jof on the financial side of the business until he died in 1973. By the time the business began to expand rapidly in 1970, Jof had virtually retired. In 1978 he died, aged seventy-five. Nick was very supportive to Fan at this sad point in her life. He was by this time divorced and took most of his meals with his mum.

By this time they had acquired a small shop in Harrogate. In the '80s Nic approached Fan with his latest expansion project, about which Fan was enthusiastic – although she vetoed some other schemes. The plan was to buy a four-floor department store building in Harrogate's main shopping area. There followed a hectic and very expensive period of refurbishment, and to exploit this huge investment fully it was necessary to diversify into jewellery, cosmetics, beauty concessions and a restaurant, as well as continuing with the core business of ladies' and gents' high-class outfitting. Nick's instincts were right. Harrogate is a wealthy spa town and a shopping centre for the 'golden triangle' between the northern suburbs of Leeds, Harrogate and Wetherby. Even in the hard years of the early 1980s, when the manufacturing districts of West Yorkshire were in serious trouble, the 'old money' was still abundant here.

Meanwhile Fan's life took yet another unexpected turn.

CHAPTER 22

A New Beginning

'But wherefore do not you a mightier way
Make war on this bloody tyrant, Time?'
William Shakespeare

In 1982 Fan was sixty-five, and a very busy elderly widow. She had a wide circle of friends and a busy social life. Among her many friends in Bradford were George Craig and his wife Maisie. George had first met Fan many years before when he was her gynaecologist. Sadly he was widowed in 1981, and absolutely out of the blue, in 1982, he asked Fan to marry him. Fan rejected his overtures, seeing him only as a loved and respected friend. She decided to take a break, leaving Nick in charge of the business, in order to travel. She visited South Africa to catch up with friends and America to see her sister.

On her return Fan picked up an unexpected phone call from George, who was operating in Sheffield: his massive reputation as a surgeon meant that his services were in demand throughout the north. He wanted to come and talk. Fan invited him to dinner, after which they retired to the sunroom for coffee, whisky and a smoke. When he proposed again Fan said, 'No, I've built a wall around myself.' The agony of being twice widowed was enough to cope with.

But George was not going to give up. The next morning Fan and Nick were in the office working on buying stock, after which they went home to Fan's for lunch and a gin and tonic. Suddenly the doorbell rang: it was George, holding a book in front of his face. It was very aptly entitled 'And the walls came tumbling down,' by Jack Fishman. George said nothing! Nick pushed Fan in the back and she fell into George's arms. He whispered, 'Would you change your mind?' 'Do I have a choice?' said Fan, laughing. 'Let's have a drink on that,' said Nick, who, despite his faults, loved his mum dearly and wanted her to be happy.

Next day they arranged to meet with the Rev. Brandon Jackson, Provost of Bradford (later Dean of Lincoln), at the cathedral. Brandon Jackson is renowned as a blunt man. He brought out the necessary forms to obtain a special licence, allowing them to marry in the cathedral quietly, without the usual delay of three weeks for the reading of the banns. The first question on the form, 'Do the families approve?', infuriated Fan, and George walked out in disgust. They decided to go to London to be married at Caxton Hall, where they thought there would be the minimum fuss. Not so! There were still lots of forms to be completed.

Shortly after the disastrous interview with Brandon Jackson, George announced, 'We're getting married on Saturday at Bradford register office. The wife of the registrar is a patient of mine, so he's willing to open up an hour early, at 8.30am.' So they were married that Saturday. Fortunately Nick and all George's four children were delighted at this rather unexpected turn of events, except that Nick objected to the dress his mum had decided to wear. She gave way and wore a pale blue suit. Everyone came, even at that time of day. George had asked the Union Club (now the Bradford Club) to cater and to supply champagne, some of which Nick and family took to the shop for all staff and customers to enjoy. It was, in Fan's words, 'A whale of a do!'

George booked a brief honeymoon at the Grand Hotel, Scarborough, and rearranged his work schedule so they could enjoy a leisurely cruise to the West Indies.

Everything seemed to be in place for a happy and trouble-free retirement for the happy couple, now aged sixty-six and sixty-seven, but in Fan's life joy and heartbreak went hand in hand.

CHAPTER 23

Joy and Heartache

'And Death unfailing will strike the blow,
Then for that reason, and for a season,
Let us be merry before we go.'
John Philpot Curran

After the euphoria of the wedding a difficult decision had to be made. Where were they to live? Some years earlier Fan and Jof had sold Smithfield House and moved to a large modern bungalow at Wharfedale Rise, near to the beauty spot of Chellow Dene. Fan was very happy in a more easily managed house with a large garden and good neighbours. It was a very popular residential area that was much favoured by the professional classes, especially the senior medical staff at Bradford Royal Infirmary, which was only half a mile away. It was also close to the girls' grammar school, which had moved there sixty years or so before, because this location on the west side of the city, had the least polluted atmosphere.

George had a large house in Park Drive, Heaton, and was reluctant to leave, especially since he might be seen as 'hanging his hat up' if he moved to Fan's. She was determined not to leave her bungalow. As you might expect Fan got her way and they set up home at Wharfedale Rise, where they were to be very happy.

George continued to work as consultant gynaecologist at Bradford Royal Infirmary, while Fan continued to play a part in her business, but with decreasing control. Despite the stresses of a busy working life they enjoyed the company of a wide circle of friends and the pleasures of travel. Fan grew very fond of her grown-up stepchildren, especially Beverley Craig (who lives not far from Fan's present home and visits her every week).

On the business front times were difficult. The recession of the early 1980s and '90s hit industry in the North of England very hard. Unemployment was high, and many long-established firms of all kinds went under. High interest rates and reduced bank lending caused serious cash flow difficulties at a time when less disposable income was available. Nick was placed under enormous stress as the banks and venture capital companies circled, calling in their debts. This stress was probably the cause of Nick's sudden death from a heart attack, in April 1991, and poor Fan was left to grieve over a much-loved son.

At this point the venture capital investors installed a new managing director. He was an accountant, with little idea of how to run a fashion business. The purchase of unsuitable stock resulted in a drop in sales, and Hewlett's lost all direction; it was ultimately sold to Hooper's in 1994.

The peaceful retirement that Fan and George had hoped to enjoy was not to last very long. When she was seventy-nine and George eighty, in 1999, George passed away. Fan's grief at being widowed for a third time can only be imagined, alone in her home and finding maintenance of the bungalow and garden increasingly onerous. But Fan is, as we have seen, very resilient. Her circle of family and friends sustained her and she tried to keep going. By 2003 she was eighty-nine and not so vigorous as she had been. Something had to be done. Apart from her failing health, she was increasingly uneasy living in Chellow Dene. Bradford had changed out of all recognition since she had arrived there in the 1950s. The professional and business population, among whom she had found her circle of friends, had for the most part moved out to Menston, Ilkley and Harrogate, while the newly prosperous Asian businessmen who had emerged from the ever-growing ethnic minority population of the city were moving into the old residential districts of Heaton and Chellow Dene.

The family encouraged Fan to seek a more suitable home in a comfortable retirement flat. Fortunately McCarthy and Stone were building one of their few developments in the North. Their 'assisted living' concept provided the benefits of complete independence with the advantage of kitchen and bathroom equipment suitable for most disabilities, alarm systems, a full-time on site estate manager, a beautiful public lounge and good restaurant facilities. The site at Bingley, only 3 miles from Fan's home, was in a pretty location, with views up the Harden Beck valley to the St Ives Estate forest and moors. It was also close to local services, including the pretty Myrtle Park just next door.

Fan moved to her new home in 2004 and very quickly settled in, making many new friends. Still driving George's old Rover, she continued to visit old friends and new around the district, and go to her hairdresser once a week. Never short of company, and fortified by her lunchtime shot of vodka and evening whisky, together with a few fags every day, she was very happy there, despite the need for regular visits to the Yorkshire clinic nearby. In 2007, as always determined to maintain her independence, she reluctantly gave up her old Rover, and bought a Honda Jazz at the age of ninety-three. Unfortunately a year later she found herself unable to comfortably manage the car and reluctantly sold it. Not to be beaten, the redoubtable FANY immediately bought an electric buggy, which in fact she never used. Meanwhile the arrival in 2007 of her first great-grandson, Jamie, filled her with delight and optimism for the future.

Unfortunately failing health in her ninety-fourth year caused Fan to reluctantly leave her cosy apartment and take up residence in Cottingley Hall nursing home nearby. Fortunately she has recovered reasonable health and has returned to something like her old form. She has somehow managed to be installed in the best room in the house, with a French window and patio on the sunny side of the garden. Surrounded by her favourite books and memorabilia, and visited by many loving friends as well as her granddaughter Jo and great-grandson, she is very happy. As the reader will imagine, she is scathing about Health and Safety rules, under which she is not supposed to walk in the grounds without a member of staff. Naturally, being Fan of the FANY, she said to the nurse, ' This is my home. I'll come and go as I please!' She does so on fine days, and enjoys a fag before returning to enjoy her pre-lunch vodka and tonic with her visitor of the day. In her ninety-second year her doctor suggested to her that she should stop smoking since it 'might shorten her life'. You can imagine her reply to that.

Epilogue

I t would be wrong to conclude this book without a final tribute to the young women of the First Aid Nursing Yeomanry who gave the best years of their lives, and in some cases died, in the defence of freedom from 1914 to 1918 and again from 1940 to 1945. Their courage, resilience, cheerful acceptance of danger, privation, stress and overwork – for no pay – makes modern feminism appear to be tame stuff.

Fan Craig (Vera Walters, Vera Aungiers, Vera Hewlett) must be almost the last survivor of her amazing generation. Like her, many of her colleagues went on to lead interesting and successful lives.

Modest and self-effacing, Fan declined an award at the end of the war, on the grounds that others she had known had done much more than her. The record of the FANY in both wars is remarkable. In the First World War decorations for bravery awarded to FANYs included seventeen Military Medals, one *Légion d'Honneur* and twenty-seven *Croix de Guerre*.

During the Second World War thirty-seven SOE female agents were parachuted into enemy-occupied Europe. Three were awarded the George Cross for bravery, two posthumously. They could not be awarded a deserved Victoria Cross since as FANY volunteers they were theoretically civilians. Of these three, Odette Halloway, Violette Szabo and Noor Inyat Khan, the latter two were among thirteen FANY agents who were caught by the Germans, tortured and cruelly executed at Ravensbrück. It is believed that they were still alive when they were put in the furnace in which gassed victims were cremated.

Odette Halloway was awarded the George Cross, the MBE and the *Légion d'Honneur*. Margaret Jackson, whom Fan succeeded as Major General Gubbins's secretary and PA for the last year of the war, had after university trained as a secretary and was fluent in French. A spell in the typing pool of the BBC was followed by the Royal Institute of International Affairs, Chatham House, before being recruited by Gubbins for SOE in 1940. On the disbandment of SOE in 1946, still aged only twenty-eight, she was awarded the MBE. She joined the Allied Commission for Austria as PA to the head of the British Political Division, and then moved to the OECD. Others who were known to Fan include Vera Atkins (believed by many to be the model for Miss Moneypenny in the James Bond novels, whose research after the war revealed the grisly fate of the slaughtered FANYs), Francis Cammaerts, Odette Halloway (Sanson), who gave Fan a silk scarf with a map of Italy which was issued to agents in the field, and Harry Rée, who later became a famous headmaster and educationalist. There were many others, too numerous to mention here.

In 1948, at St Paul's Church, Knightsbridge, a memorial was unveiled by Princess Alice, Countess of Athlone, Commandant in Chief of the Women's' Transport Service (FANY), commemorating fifty-two FANYs who fell in various theatres of war, including those killed at Ravensbrück: 'There is no formula by which to calculate how much of cold courage was embodied in these thirteen women, or what they endured in dying for their countries.'

Appendices

Bibliography

Gubbins and SOE, Peter Wilkinson and Joan Bright Astley (Leo Cooper, 1993, paperback Pen and Sword, 1997)

Baker Street Irregulars, Bickham Sweet-Escott (Methuen, 1965)

In Obedience to Instructions: FANY with SOE in the Mediterranean, Margaret Pawley (Leo Cooper, 1997)

Rome 44: The Battle for the Eternal City, Raleigh Trevelyan (Secker and Warburg, 1981, paperback Pimlico, 2004)

SOE in France, M.R.D. Foot (HMSO, 1996)

Memories of an SOE Historian, M.R.D. Foot (Pen and Sword, 2008)

Memories

Fan's summary of her life was written in May 1994 for her family.

Your great-grandfather came from Monmouthshire. There was some gossip of events the wrong side of the blanket with local 'grandees' ... He was reputed to have ill-treated his wife, mother of William Walters, Augustus Walters and George Herbert Walters. The three brothers took their mother to London and looked after her for the rest of her life.

William I remember nothing about.

Augustus married someone called Lena (whom your mother was named after), and they visited us occasionally when we lived in Hadley, Hertfordshire. George Herbert married Florence Palmer, who was very petite and taught music – she was an accomplished pianist. George was very handsome with black curly hair and brilliant blue eyes. They produced George Augustus William (1900), Lena Florence (1907) and Vera Muriel, me (1914).

Florence Palmer, our mother, died in 1922. George worked in the Westminster bank and Len left the local grammar school to work in a local dress shop! I drifted around an empty house, as our father wasn't exactly paternalistic, until brother George warned our father we could be in trouble if I was not sent to school: education was compulsory. So I went to a small private school in Finchley where we read excerpts from Shakespeare and walked the park in crocodiles, but I don't remember much else – which explains a lot!

George married Violet and produced Vivien. Both George and Violet died two years ago.

Len married Nick Endacott, with you as the result.

After a chequered career, Father said I was to stay at home and run the house. I had other ideas, so took a secretarial course and had two jobs before I married Norman Aungiers. Norman was a lieutenant in the TA Artists Rifles, and died of an aneurysm whilst training on Salisbury Plain in 1939.

Your grandfather was one of the founders of colour printing and lectured at the London School of Printing, although his job was at John Swain, who were well-known printers and had their works in Barnet, where he was from 1890 to 1958. He remarried someone called May in 1945. She died in 1952.

Fan in Algeria, 1943

F an was bound by the Official Secrets Act, of course, and in her letters to and from her sister Lena no mention could be made of her work for SOE, or any other military matters. Nor could or would she reveal any discomfort or fear that she might have felt. For example, in the first letter to her sister and father she does not point out that she and her eleven FANY colleagues were travelling on an overcrowded troopship and in serious danger of attacks by U-boats. The only clue as to her whereabouts in her second letter is the mention of 'the French'. She was of course in Algeria, then a French colony. In the third letter there are some hints of discomfort and overwork, despite which she 'doesn't want to be back home just yet for all the tea in China'.

The final letter in this group describes in graphic detail a brief spell of leave spent exploring the Atlas Mountains in winter. At this stage Fan is still excited by her work, her promotion to officer status and occasional social events. Only later do we sense her exhaustion and sometimes depression, which she seeks to hide in letters home.

En route to Algiers, 1942

Dearest Pops & May,

Just a hurried note on board to let you know we are living in absolute luxury as first-class passengers – in fact apart from the lifebelt it's rather difficult to imagine we are not in London still – the whole thing now seems so very unreal.

The main item of news – egg and bacon breakfast – steak and chips lunch- chicken dinner – butter unlimited – the navy know how to live.

The 'pips' are now up [on her shoulder, denoting officer status] – in fact altogether I am having great difficulty in believing this is really me. So Pop you have nothing to worry about and Lena will let you know as soon as we arrive – I have no idea when that will be – but I shall write again as soon as I get there. This letter will be sent you by the censor sometime after we have sailed.

We have an E.N.S.A party on board [professional entertainers volunteering for the front line] – I do admire them trailing around the world to entertain troops – can't be a real comfortable existence!

That whisky and brandy are going to be even more welcome than I imagined as the ship is 'dry' – it's a nice feeling to have it on me if anything should happen. I am only allowed three letters so if you are on the phone to George wish them goodbye for me- and every success to the home guard!!! (I heard so much about it over our drink last Saturday)

Please write to me soon – any old scraps of news – although they are the grandest crowd (we are twelve in all) by the time we reach our destination our own friends are going to seem a long way away.

Much love to you both
Vera

Letter to Fan's in-laws from Massingham (Algiers)

F.A.N.Y
Massin V.Algiers
Inter Services Signal Unit 6
B.N.A.F
31 May 43

Dearest all,

I have first to thank you for several letters, news from home is terrifically welcome – you can imagine the clamour when the mail comes into the mess, whilst I think of it would you let me have Margaret's address I would love to know what part of this coast she is in now, yesterday we had (we being another FANY, the Major for whom I toil and myself) a perfect opportunity to see French family life, we were invited to lunch and to stay the afternoon at their home which is built on piles on the cliffside, in fact they dive off the veranda straight into the sea. It was the most amazing afternoon, we started lunch at 1.15 and ate solidly for two and a half hours, not allowed to refuse anything (I couldn't help thinking of Mummy A' digestion!!) you need a complete vacuum inside to cope with eating here, we had 8 courses each accompanied by a different wine from our host's vineyards – finishing the meal with large slices of very sweet fruit cake, black coffee and rum, – just stupefied with food we thought we would probably just sit back and snooze, but no, our host who is very round and seated at the head of the table with his napkin tucked in his collar and his hat on, ordered the table to be taken away and produced a violin to which he would take no excuses for one's inability to dance (all this in the sort of heat you can't imagine at home). But what is so amazing about the French, they seem so slack compared to English homes and yet the 'finesse' about everything is perfect – knowing just what two things to eat together or what to drink with what; first entertaining their guests without you feeling it is an effort on anyone's part – they make you so completely welcome – our host's knowledge of English art and poetry our hostesses' what seemed endless gifts for needlework, singing, leather work etc. completely amazed us. The afternoon was finished bathing off the rocks whilst our host played the accordion, and a gift of a painting done by a fellow guest (a Frenchman) for each of us and an invitation to the feast of Pentecost. I might add we didn't face dinner in the mess last night – had a feeling we might not want to eat again. I have mumbled on and now finished this up without telling you all the news but will write again.

Letter to in-laws from Massingham on being promoted to ensign (FANY equivalent of lieutenant)

Dearest Pop and May,

News of you and only 8 days old – I do wish we were allowed more of these air letters for they are the only interesting way to write, sea letters take so long – we only have one of these a week. Terribly disappointed to hear about the slacks for mosquitoes certainly like me, although so far, the camp has been lucky and we have only had one or two malaria cases. We are most terribly busy now, and the heat and my Major (my boss) in bed ill, all conspire to make life rather difficult, but it is all so interesting that I wouldn't want to be back home just yet for all the tea in China, apart from a leave in which to see you again. Have you had my SOS re coupons for shirts, I'm sorry it was such a scrappy airgraph [airmail letter], but a 'flap' was on at the time so it was written in great haste. We have a terrific number of Fannies out here now, all privates, corporals and sergeants, and to my horror I was detailed to take six of them to a dance – (I to be officer in charge) this fairly shook me as previously I have managed, through being a secretary to steer clear of the military side of FANY life – by the way, whilst on this topic – did I tell you my commission had been confirmed – this sounds a bit 'Georgeish' [slang term for conceited] – but I do feel so terrifically bucked about it!! My French lessons have faded out as I have had to work every afternoon, as well as do a course in ciphering and other army horrors! Did you and May have a good, though short holiday. All the news I have of Jools sounds good, thank heaven all that adenoids business is over. I had a letter from her – written by herself. I'm sending you some fruit in the next mail. Do you think you and Lena could do something about some slacks for me in khaki, it wouldn't matter about a top if they were the material of my uniforms – if only we had been told this before we left England. Another item, knowing May's 'acquiring' habits if you ever have any soap – the clothes washing sort to spare, it would help lots, we have a women to wash our clothes but there is no soap in this country and we have to scrounge to get our shirts washed.

With much love to you both
Vera

A rare spell of leave while at Massingham – Fan is writing to her sister Lena

My dearest Len,

Today here's two air letters for you as we have had an extra one as a 'treat' and because I have heaps to tell you having just returned from seven days leave and what a leave. To start with I believe I told you about my 'Woofly' Major in an earlier letter, he had previously suggested taking me on a trip of as much as possible of North Africa. So I jumped at it (first of all persuading another FANY to take her leave the same time. Woofles was a pet, he provided another chappie to help Dorothy evened up, and away we went with batman [officer's servant] and chauffeur , to be utterly feted and pampered for seven days. The first day was most eventful, crisp and sunny, we drove off to the mountains, eventually arriving at lunch time at Fort Nationale, a real walled fort on the top of a mountain populated by real Arabs who stood and gazed at Dorothy and I (we weren't sure if it was for our appearance value or something on top of the arch). After lunch we continued along the mountain road climbing all the time, until suddenly we ran into real deep snow, the car took a sudden lurch to the side and we prayed our hardest and most fervently ever, for as it slithered across the snow, it went towards the precipice and we really thought we had had it. So there we stayed for one and a half hours in a terrific snow storm, not knowing what to do, afraid to start the car in case she went right over. Then to our relief when we had visions of our skeletons possibly being found next spring, some Arabs appeared with donkeys laden with their household goods, they informed us they were evacuating the villages higher up until the spring and that we would never get through, with that they prepared to leave us to our fate. Almost on bended knee they were prevailed upon to lift the car back on to the road and so the car was pushed backwards down the mountain to the village, with us trailing through the snow. Anyway it all worked out marvellously, we arrived to find a really nice hotel and the nearest to a Swiss scene I shall ever see, Hotel after the Holiday Inn idea surrounded by fir trees and snow topped mountains. Next day – just had present from nice Captain of six pairs of silk stockings from Italy – so am including another pair in your Christmas parcel. I'm also sending by sea today a letter containing a cheque for Susan as there is absolutely nothing out here for children – not even sandals now, so would you buy something for her – In a letter I had from [indecipherable] he said he helped to get a bookcase for her bedroom perhaps this will help.

To get back to the leave, if you can find a map, you will get some idea of the country we went through in our 400 mile journey – going east from Algiers through the valleys, between real snow capped mountain ranges, valleys out here are not a bit like home, there are really vast plains without any trees in fact hardly any greenery. The only signs of life is occasional brick huts and Arabs ploughing with their odd assorted teams of mules, horses and oxen. The road passes through scattered villages hotch potch of French and Arab, mostly very dirty and through the most picturesque gorges. We spent the next night in a town called Setif, very cold and very dirty. Arabs were very intrigued with Dorothy and I when we went for a walk whilst our escorts were busy until we joined them for black coffee and brandy, the mid morning custom here. Then on to the lovely town of Constantine which was built by the Phoenicians (can't spell it) in the bowl formed by a ring of mountains with a deep gorge right through the centre of the town. Even the Arab quarters are most picturesque, all blue or white in the sunshine. From the moment we arrived Dorothy and I were thoroughly feted immediately, made guests for all meals at the garrison officers mess – it was a really farcical (one's popularity I'm afraid cannot be credited to our personalities but merely being the only two British women there other than two rather ancient nurses). One evening we got in such a mess having accepted invitations to dine with two Colonels, four Majors and a Captain at different places that we had to confess and make a combined party in one of their flats, but this was all very tricky as D held the Major's hand all through dinner and the Colonel on the other side got snooty and walked out as he happened to be the Major's boss – situation decidedly awkward. This at home sounds childish but out here most men are odd one way or another. Hot weather, lack of lime juice and all that!! My last day of leave Woofles and I went to [censored] near the town .

Naples to Rome, 1944

By the beginning of 1944 Fan had been working eighteen hours a day, with increasing responsibilities for almost three years. During 1943 she had no home leave and no break apart from the trip to the Atlas Mountains. The year culminated in the invasion of Sicily and then mainland Italy. By now she had been appointed ADC to Colonel Dodds-Parker, CO of SOE in Italy and the Mediterranean area. She was now in a fearful warzone, under great stress and at times in danger, while her senior role isolated her from her female friends and colleagues, and she was missing home and family; yet these feelings only rarely show amid mundane domestic and family chat. As she remarks, 'I'm far too disgustingly healthy to be sent home for a rest'.

Fan's letter to her sister soon after she and her colonel arrived in Naples is full of the excitement and adventure involved in the invasion and the promise that it held of eventual victory. The 'luxury liner' she mentions is an Italian fishing boat with a crew who rather frightened Fan and her pal Leanora Railton who accompanied her. Her colonel was flown across the Mediterranean by the RAF. Her excitement at her first taste of Italy hides the reality of cold, hunger, hardship and non-stop work. Even her brief spell in Cairo is made to sound like a jolly holiday trip – but the reality was rather different. Her terrifying flight across Crete (still in German occupation) to Athens (liberated hours before) is described as a 'wonderful opportunity'.

The letter from Brindisi to her sister marks her promotion to captain in the FANY, the equivalent of major in regular Army rankings. On Colonel Dodds-Parker's return to London she had become ADC to Major-General Stawell, and something of her distaste at his very different 'old school' military style comes through.

Fan's letter in November from Naples betraying her homesickness is lightened only by her second meeting with Jof Hewlitt, who was to be her second husband after the war. She can say nothing of the horrors of the battle of Monte Casino, and her arrival in Rome hours after the Germans left.

Her next letter again hints of homesickness, and the possibility that Hewlett could be her means of escape.

By December Fan is again hinting at her unhappiness with her new boss, despite greater comfort and a visit to Sienna. Her tentative courtship with Hewlitt continues.

Visit of the FANY CO from England to Massingham

Dearest Len,

Can't help feeling awfully worried about you when I haven't had a letter from you for over a week now that we seem to hear constant news of raids on London, begin to wish you were ground floor in Putney still!

Anyway I hope by the time this reaches you my 'boss' will have rung you up (he is three weeks in London) and I shall have first hand news of you on his return.

News is nil Len – having a bad week, constant fit of depression, homesickness and vaccinations and dislike of the office without my boss, in fact just b.....y minded! What I'd like is a trip home for about four weeks, tried to persuade my boss it was a good thing for me to be dehydrated and come back in a despatch case, but he was afraid he might forget to soak me in water at the other end so here I remain. I think the real cause of the general 'browned offness' in the camp is the cold. For the first ten to fourteen days it has rained really torrents, blown a gale and been intensely cold. I can't imagine why people spend a fortune in wintering in the Mediterranean.

Is Susan having a party on Sunday? I had hoped to send her some fruit but haven't been into town for weeks. What is the position now Len regarding her? Can she come to the flat when ever you want her?

We have had the 'Queen B' FANY (Gamwell, CO of FANY) staying here the last few days so we have all been painfully 'booted and spurred', dressed for dinner, impeccable mess manners, the strain something terrific. She really is the most amazing personality, frightfully inspiring.

From Massingham: the loneliness of Fan's job as ADC to Colonel Dodds-Parker

Dearest Len,

My 'boss' returned today convinced there is no such place as 23 [Len's address] – says I have Mediterranean madness and probably you live in Brighton! He was really very funny about his trot round the back streets looking for 23. I was awfully sorry you didn't see him particularly as it is more than likely I shall 'stooge' Ma for him for all time – at least these seem to be his plans at present. This is one of these stages when I would desperately much like to talk to you, the old career versus poor but happy raises its ugly head nearer and nearer!

I still haven't heard about the visit to Ma, was it such that words cannot describe it. [Indecipherable] sent me some photos of Susan – when is she going to have a band round her teeth Len – surely it should be sometime soon or has the idea been abandoned?

Life is beginning to get really lonely these days, all the old FANYS are being posted elsewhere, all the officers who used to form the parties we went on last summer and autumn have moved – but I begin to feel I'm here forever. My job as Colonel's stooge divorces me from the rest of the camp – all too 'high level!' So you see how desperate the longing for the old chin wag becomes and I'm far too disgustingly healthy to be sent home for a spell of rest as one of the girls is doing.

Douglas (Dodds-Parker) came back with reports of lots of bangs around your way – Len – do you think you should there – I've horrible fear, knowing you, that you stay up on that top floor, however bad it is.

Went to another party on board a weeny (small) ship with one of the Cornwall 'chappies' last Saturday, there were four Majors, the naval type and five FANYs, dinner was super finishing with strawberries and cream. After dinner, the hatches above the cabin were opened and two of the sailors played the bag pipes on the deck – we being all just nicely oiled for singing purposes – let it go – oh that walk down a swaying gang plank afterwards! Anyway,it was a good party.

Really getting down to letter writing tonight – duty officer so have to stay up until 12.30. Much love.

Fan arrives in Italy, having moved on to Naples as ADC to Dodds-Parker.

Dearest Len,
Never a dull moment – here we are in that place which one is advised to see and die [Naples] – I started a letter to you a few days ago on board a luxury liner [fishing boat] in mid-Mediterranean but had to give up, the heat was such that it took every ounce of energy to lie on your bunk and do nothing – concentrated thought was out of the question. This is somewhat reminiscent of my West Country job (except for Mac) as well as tackle the office, I have to run what is now our home – the staff is Italian and as I haven't the vaguest idea what they are talking about we are getting along fine. My pretty FANY help about which I wrote you is also here and she, Dorothy and I live in an enormous furnished flat on the hills overlooking the much talked of bay – the window of the room in which I am writing this to you looks out across the bay to the mountain which created such newspaper interest a few weeks ago [Vesuvius]. I'm so thrilled at seeing these places that sometimes Len it's a job to believe it's really me and that actually I am back in the flat with you. We were sorry to leave our chums at the other place for it would be very difficult to find any complaints against our existence there but it is fun to be a

tiny unit again away from camp life.

You may have had all this news already as my heart-throb No. 1 arrived at the old place the evening before we left intending to stay a few days before returning home – oh was I mad having stayed in that place for 15 months without moving – I have to leave the very weekend I would have liked to stay – anyway he saw us off in fact without his help coping with our mountains of luggage as Leo (the FANY) and I travelled alone, I think we should still be on the docks now. Anyway as soon as he reaches London he is coming to see you – I fear it's a misplaced heartthrob. In spite of the apparent interest, as the level is very stratospheric – I believe I told you his name is Kenneth Greenlees (Major) Cameronians – takes it for granted the rest of the world that he knows is of equal blue blood!! That my dear sis, is how it stands at the moment – a mutual admiration society – but an impossible level for me to attain in spite of my present training. Again you will probably have gathered all this long before you receive this letter.

The next day – my yesterday's attempt was broken off by the arrival of two naval types I knew in the West Country – it's rather fun this running up against odd people in odd places. They whisked Leo and I off to the local club for dinner – apparently everywhere you go here you wallow in music – orchestras and opera singers really let themselves go – last night having let off considerable steam in the classical world, they got going on the dance music which they really can play so feeling thoroughly conspicuous in this enormous restaurant all mirrors and gold leaf and only one other British girl there, a nurse, Leo and I and the naval types danced to shouts of 'Come on British show them how'!!

There is no difficulty in falling for this country in fact I wish so much I could transplant you here onto this balcony this morning, I think you would feel the same way – but the local inhabitants! Our domestic staff couldn't be more helpful but somehow you cannot quite forget that 10 months ago they were the other end of the axis [Italy-German Alliance] and that these girls with their liquid brown eyes were gazing on the Jerry in exactly the same way as they are now looking on the British and American soldiers – it needs getting used to.

I have heard that it is possible to buy material in this town – if this is so I'll get around in the hope of sending some home to you in time for the trousseau.

I'm writing to Pop and Mrs. A re my new address but if you get this first would you give them a ring. We feel rather cut off at present as it will probably take ages for our mail to catch up with us, in fact we haven't yet located our office equipment and the car hasn't arrived so we are more or less confined to the flat. Conscience says this time should be spent learning Italian but somehow Leo and I keep finding ourselves dozing in the sun merely rousing ourselves to admire this perfect view – it's so wonderful not to have any files or office for a while after the last few months.

Len, I don't suppose your D. agrees but the times I've wished you had joined the FANY with me are innumerable – we could have liked seeing some of these places together – not to mention the incredible good fortune of doing all this and being paid for it and as at present 'doing' for the nicest man in the world – I can't help thinking how well you would have run this place with all its high level entertaining. As it is I grope along knowing where I am in the office but getting hotter and more dry-mouthed every minute coping with D's contacts and trying to live up to the job he has put me on.

Big hug each for Toots and Douglas and much love to you V.

In Cairo with Dodds- Parker

My dearest Len,

Ages since I heard from you and at the rate I'm whizzing around the Mediterranean, I begin to wonder if I'll ever catch up with anything again. My birthday was celebrated by twelve hours in an aeroplane with a very queasy tummy after eating spam at a spot in North Africa. So my boss decided the day should be celebrated in better style elsewhere at a later date and in a party we wined and dined off all the luxuries the world can produce in a super night club in Cairo. I can't begin to describe the town to you – the one word 'luxury' is synonymous with Cairo – you barely breathe for yourself without a black servant rushing at you to help. It would be cruel to describe the food and the drink – I'll tell you in leave time! I slept on a house boat on the Nile in the same style as everything else. Actually it is a most exciting place to visit but would be thoroughly demoralising (not to mention the expense) – permanent residents seem to reach a stage when they are incapable of thinking for themselves except to be spiteful about each other. There is everything imaginable in the shops, the prices are impossible but I hope to send you something from here. Since writing so far the most frightful thing has happened – one of the girls asked me to have her gold watch repaired whilst I am here and I have lost it – that will put me back months of pay as a gold watch is an incredible price and I'll have to replace it.

Sunday my boss declared a holiday and we went sight seeing – saw the pyramids, the Sphinx (whose chin is propped up with sandbags as a war time measure) and the various famous temples in the desert – finishing with tea at the famous Mena House hotel to see the wealthy Egyptians' social life and had my future told me by an incredibly ancient Arab who made signs in the sand, – bags of joy for ever more!!!!

Love V.

Brief visit to Athens – six weeks after the Germans left

My Dearest Len,

I sometimes pinch myself to think it is really me that has had these wonderful opportunities as you gathered from my last letter I had 'got round' a bit and since then and in complete contrast I have been to Greece and seen those people who have suffered so much at the hands of the Germans. One morning my 'boss' did not need me so I went for a walk through a famous town [Athens] – it's difficult to describe the emotion and my embarrassment at the welcome of the people – they clutched my hands as I walked along, patted my back, everyone smiled and stared and my photograph was taken three times in the space of ten minutes walk. They had already greeted British men but a British woman seemed to be too much. As I walked into my hotel bedroom two chamber maids were making the bed – to my amazement they rushed at me, tears streaming down their faces, smothered me in kisses, it is so embarrassing for they are still hungry and until the machinery is set in motion and food is brought into the country one feels ashamed of being so well fed. The shops are full of the lovelies and things which have been hidden away during the occupation but the prices are in the billion drachma region as money has gone haywire here so nothing can be bought. The atmosphere of relief that pervades the place is impossible to put on paper – welcome is written on every wall and pictures of Churchill are in every shop window – it is all an experience I shall never forget. Our aeroplane had a Greek Jew who couldn't do enough. He must have another sweet and some tea .He must not have seen his country and his wife for four and a half years – he was so excited as we came into land – he laughed and wept alternately then hugged us all in turn. One feels very 'little' in face of the courage of these people – please heaven we as a nation never do anything ... [The remainder of this letter is no longer legible.]

Brindisi, Italy: Dodds-Parker returns home ill

Dearest Len,

Events have moved so rapidly I'm breathless – East Italy, Egypt, Greece, three 'pips', [promoted to captain],series of high level, terrifically interesting lunch and dinner parties, endless meetings and you have the last three weeks. Today I dine with Kenneth Greenlees, who has turned up here again. By here I mean East Italy as I still haven't got back to one's roost yet.

I'm so glad Rollo Seddon saw you – I thought you would like him – I do wish you had met Kenneth. Douglas (Dodds-Parker) I'm not surprised you haven't seen as he was more than determined to get his heart problem straightened out when he left. Fame and career are his goal in life and a FANY with no background however devoted he was did not fit in.

I would so love to tell you of the people we met in the places we have just visited but it will all have to wait the depressing thought is that no one here thinks we shall be home until well into Spring or Summer. A few old timers including myself have been asked to write our personal memoirs – it's damn difficult for things that have been terrifically thrilling to me, not having been anywhere before, are probably as dull as dish water to anyone else.

Your party sounded absolutely terrific – frightfully jolly. However did you get 31 people in that room – yes three of you ...

I heard today from [??? – another suitor] saying matrimony was off – I can't see [???] and I with a cat and canary yet! Whilst in a tremulous voice I recount my doings as a 'girl' in North Africa.....!

Rollo hasn't returned yet but thank you heaps for the shirt and birthday present.

Do you ever ring up Mrs A, only I feel I give you more news than anyone as it's so difficult to find time to write.

I wish I liked my new job more but it's somehow so intangible after the last – dancing attendance on the almighty [Major General Stawell, her new boss] organising his travelling and his programmes, tucking the rug round his knees in the flame, going to his meetings – there's nothing to get your teeth into and the tact required to overcome the prejudice against a woman ADC strains my resources to the uttermost – I wonder if I'll stick it.

Love to you both , Vera

Fan revisits Naples after moving to Rome through the Monte Cassino battlefield

Dearest Len,

I hope by now you have had all the latest news from Betty Sale as she should have arrived in UK a week ago.

Len, how absolutely frightful losing your coat. I didn't imagine the insurance money is much help without coupons, or even the equivalent coat in the shops. Is there any hope of getting it back – I imagine not? Terrifically glad to hear you are getting up to see [???] it must be months since she saw any of her 'ain folk' folk.

I am writing this in the Naples villa – I like coming back here for I have my kit and comfy bed here but it makes me frightfully nostalgic over dear old Douglas. My 'boss' and I are leaving for Rome and the North – I shall certainly know my Italy after this job. Len, it is strange, I love going places, my boss is a dear, and I have all the luck but none of these things counteract the homesickness of the last three or four weeks – I feel I've 'had' this overseas business –

no doubt as soon as I get home I'd long to go places again but I'd give anything to come home for a while.

I had dinner with my widower [Lt.-Col. Hewlett] last evening – suddenly out of the blue, over coffee, he said 'after my training as ADC to a general would I be prepared to look after a mere Lieutenant Colonel for the rest of my life' – I stalled on this one! Never a dull moment!! [This was his first proposal of marriage.] November 16th Rome – in the most amazing villa – built during the war by a wealthy fascist, all in highly polished wood and marble – I thought I'd seen some film settings in my moves but this out Hollywoods Hollywood – electric buttons everywhere which do everything, open windows, shut doors etc – give me a home!!!

Mrs Aungiers has also written to say her gloves were too small, if I can get out I will try to buy some more while I'm in Rome. Did she tell you Margaret [censored] had married recently, in Palestine [illegible].

I'd give anything for a 'back home' down with you Len, my new job has a very much more entertaining side which it would not be polite to write down [this refers to her boss's indiscretions] – I have never even imagined myself in the role of straight laced housemaid – yet here I am!!

Love to you both V.

Fan dines out with Jof Hewlitt, and is seriously considering his proposal

Dearest Len and Douglas,
This is grand, a letter one day from D and the next from you Len. Len our twin souls must be working again – or rather our tummies as the day you fell ill – was the day we were motoring across Italy and the mountain roads are so high and so cold and twisty that it was more than the innards would take and to my horror (and the General's!) I was well and truly sick – the newest low of embarrassment! Len I hope to goodness you are fit again now, as some time has lapsed – I've memories of some of the bilious attacks

you can manage and you always did the job so thoroughly. Anyway I feel you are in the best possible hands. Give him a hug from me.

Feel awfully disappointed about L's news. I thought she really was going to take the plunge this time: – as you say what a gal!

Most of my news you have already had as I wrote to you from Rome. He (the General) 'hobnobbed' in a big way when there but frankly I just didn't 'take on' with these folk whatever strata, and the superficial gush of bonhomie which is necessary is frightfully wearing. None of these things tend to make me like the job which is mainly official/social, and the strain of organising high powered lunches and dinners!! I'm always so tempted to consider who I would like to sit next to instead of what order they should sit in relation to the 'boss'. All this is tending to drive me more and more to John [Jof Hewlett], the widower, as the means of escape from the high level whenever we get to Naples. Things reached a new nadir last night when Jof took me to the mess for dinner, two and a half hours of this was as much as we could take so Jof and I escaped to the local club to dance and drink and leave 'higher levels' to uninterrupted petting parties – what a life!!

I can't imagine what has happened to Betty Sale as no one has heard of her arrival in UK and she should have been with you on about the 8th of the month. She has some sandals for Susan's and Vivien's Christmas stockings which I bought in Cairo. I managed to get another pair of gloves in Rome for Mrs A but most of the stuff in this country is such trash it is not worth buying. I'm still hoping though to come across something really worth while on my travels for you two to have as a memento of the day.

Incidentally I'm considering the prospect of saying 'yes' to Jof so you may be saved the problem of an old maid sister in law. It's only considering.

Much love V.

Fan visits Sienna

Dearest D and Len,

I gather you must be whole again Len as in the letter I had yesterday (isn't it marvellous letters only taking 3/4 days) you were having a baking day. That and your description of the flat made me terrifically homesick. I do agree most wholeheartedly with all you say about other people always wanting the other person's job etc. And it is a problem ... all the girls that have been out here sometime, jobs closing down and the constant bad throats and tummies we all have here have the most depressing effect. But my problem is to adjust myself (and like it) from the 'idealist' to the 'earthly', for where, as we are, one is tied all waking hours to the person for whom you work – the type makes all the difference. The biggest of all consolations – we do get around – and in comfort!

We went to Sienna last week and then we were to go to Florence but much to my woe I managed to run a temperature and was left behind in Sienna. Sienna is just like a medieval fairy story or a Shakespeare setting for the 'household' clashes in Romeo and Juliet. It is just as it must have been 600 years ago. If you shut your eyes against the jeeps, army lorries and uniforms you can imagine the scenes when the rival households met in Sienna main square.

On each trip I am a little more amazed by this country – there can hardly be anywhere else in the world where there is so much breathtaking beauty and such utter degradation and squalor mixed together. The language when you hear it is Rome and Sienna is the most musical imaginable. By the way talking of rain – never believe the posters of 'sunny Italy'.

I'm absolutely staggered that Betty hasn't appeared as she was so very grateful at being given somewhere where she could stay and not only that she has Susan's and Vivien's Cairo sandals. I'm worried something might have happened to her as it is so unlike her in every way and I've known her intimately for a year. I had been told to go to [possibly Rome] for a wedding present so I'm still hoping.

Spending the day with the widower tomorrow – will report later!

Much love V.

Letters from Fan's friend 'V', based in Germany after VE Day, 1945

These letters were sent to Fan by her friend after Fan's return to England and the end of her service in the FANY.

V was working with the British Army of the Rhine (BAOR), which occupied part of Germany as the war ended. Because the war has ended V is able to describe in graphic detail conditions in defeated Germany, and the horrific revelations of concentration camps, including Dachau. She also visits Berchtesgarten, Hitler's mountain retreat, and Linz, where he planned to construct a new capital city for the Reich.

16th July 1945

My dear Vera

Well, here is the beginning of the first instalment. We had a very good trip really, even though we did start at crack of dawn and I had to spend the last night on an Army bed at the hostel. Of course about halfway across the pilot told us that we were not landing where we were expected, as we arrived transport less, and had to make our way in company with thousands of ATS, some of whom were apparently those who walked out when ENSA made cracks about comforts for the troops.

Our first lunch had to be seen to be believed. I've never known such an atmosphere in my life. The whole place seemed to be split up into rival factions, all making cracks under their breaths at the others, while we four sat feeling rather new and out of our depth. Perhaps they didn't notice, I hope not, but I was expecting it so listened hard! and learnt quite a lot. Most of the trouble seems to be because Van, who is CO, hasn't sufficient personality to make himself felt, leaving room for everyone else to double cross in the usual race – for what? Whilst my boss had divorced himself from everyone else completely to be able to carry on his own work which bears no relation to that of the others, and consists, at present, in carrying on where Dumbo and the others left off, and there is an amazing amount still left to be done, which means that I go along too. At the moment he's planning a trip, rather on the lines of Leo's, though not on such a high level! Which should be fascinating.

However, since then the atmosphere seems to be better, or I'm getting used to it. Perhaps it's feminine influence!

We're installed, as I think I told you, at a place called Bad Salzsuflen near Hanover in three houses, one for us, one for the men, and one to work in. One used to be a doctor's house and the other two were pensions. This used to be a spa, and is filled with either one or the other. It's really very pretty, and the houses are more nearly French than anything else I know with very high sloping roofs, and really very comfortable, though I believe ours is the only one with hot water!

We have a German cook who is really excellent, and we're getting fat on butter, eggs and very well cooked food. Don't ask me where it comes from, I've no idea, though the meat is often unidentifiable. There are two other German girls who come in and clean and make our beds and so on. Two of them are very friendly, the cook particularly, the other rather stiff and formal, and some how much more to one's respect, if not liking.

I've not seen many Germans so far, but the ones I have seen seem quite well dressed and well fed, though this village is no criterion of the towns of Germany. If you pass them in the street they take no notice of you, and you take no notice of them.

It's difficult to know what one feels about non-fraternisation once one is here, though that is lifted now. It's difficult not to feel friendly to all the world when the country is lovely and the sun is shining, however little you may show it, and you begin to feel that something constructive must be done for the future. I think non-fraternisation was a very good thing, and had given everyone time to grow and think more clearly of what is to be done.

We do live in a compound, that is to say, the area is bound by barbed wire, but as far as I know, we are allowed out in twos as far as we can walk in any direction. There's not, at present, much to do, there's a cinema, and a very nice swimming bath – open air – and they talk of opening an officers' club but that hasn't so far materialized. Fortunately two of the other ones who came out with us already knew people out here, so they've been able to amuse themselves quite satisfactorily and settle down rather better than they would otherwise have done, and I think we shall all get ourselves organised soon.

I'll have to end the first instalment here I'm afraid, how are you? Have you had a second to relax, and are your protégés alright, not to mention the General's cushions? Give my love to Joan if you see her, and write and tell me all the gossip.

Lots of love

V.

In Germany as the war ends

How can I begin to describe without being dreary, all that I saw and felt during the three and a half weeks we were away. It would fill a book, but I'm afraid it's not in me to bring it to life. However I'll try, and if I fail I'm sorry.

Landmarks of course stand out, but so much is forgotten, that perhaps it's better to describe them than to try to follow the route and put in things which in comparison seem dull.

The first impressions were the desolation and destruction which war and bombing have brought to Germany. It is almost impossible to describe what the big towns like Karlsruhe, Kassel, Darmstadt, Pforzheim, where it took us an hour and a half to find the road out, look like, for there is nothing with which you can compare them, unless you can imagine whole towns looking like the City [of London] did immediately after the raids, mile upon mile of streets which you cannot enter, ruined buildings, which show no sign of having ever been occupied, wallpaper stripped from the walls, no broken furniture lying about or fittings showing where a fireplace had been, nothing but piles of bricks and rubble, in some cases even with weeds already growing over them. Towns the size of Farnborough with not one house standing, villages in the middle of nowhere razed to the ground. Frankfurt, where only the colossal I.G. Farben factory, now SHAEF HQ, with its marble pillars, polished floors, beautiful gardens and fountains – surely the ideal factory – reigns supreme and untouched over a city which has lost its Cathedral all but the spire, the opera, the Rathaus, the Romme, dating from Charlemagne's days; Mannheim Ludwigshafen with its temporary bridges across the Rhine; Worms where the statue of Martin Luther stands before a ruined Cathedral – 'Hier bleibe ich, ich kann night anders' ['Here I stay, I can do no other': Martin Luther] – and the rest of the town is rubble.

On to our first concentration camp – a filthy conglomeration of buildings in the middle of a dusty road, now housing Wehrmacht or SS with pile upon pile of records presided over by a hawk faced French woman, which would take months to go through.

Down to Baden Baden, which is disappointing, through the Black Forest by the top road, mile upon mile of tall pines, steep sided valleys, blue, blue lakes surrounded by trees and glorious views to Lake Constance with the Swiss Alps in the distance; none of them with snow at this time of year, but invigorating and beautiful and clean, clean villages and streams, white bricks, white sails on the lake so that you forget the war, until you come to Friedrichshafen where they used to build zeppelins and now must rebuild their town.

Then up to Munich, the most tragic city of them all; so little damaged comparatively, but terribly battered, making one regret more than anywhere the treasures which are lost to the world, because here you can see a little of what they were.

Dachau next: I will not believe that one could have lived near it, and not known what went on. The camp stands surrounded by trees at the end of a broad avenue with a huge entrance surmounted by the German eagle. Along the road to the right unmistakable barracks stretch for about a mile now occupied by the Americans. It was raining and a wireless was playing the Warsaw Concerto – perhaps as a funeral march to the Polish girl, who because she would not strip before the guards, was thrown alive into one of the furnaces somewhere just behind the barracks where one cannot go and where now, thousands of SS men are imprisoned, thousands too of prisoners are still there, too ill to be moved. We had lunch in what had been the guards' mess, a wood panelled room in the basement. We left soon afterwards, the records are too vast for us to go through them in less than a fortnight.

That afternoon we were shown over a German jail. It was spotless, and apparently a model one, with large windows, shining floors (I couldn't think what to do with my cigarette end!), huge clean kitchens and flowers, surely an ideal way to spend the Government's time.

In Landshut we went over the Schloss with its beautiful chapel, balcony with a sprung tiled floor where Napoleon had looked out, where the boat was kept not by water by lions, and where Angus and an American slept in Mad Ludwig of Bavaria's bed trying unsuccessfully to raise ghosts of the past.

South again this time, really into the mountains, to Garmisch Partenkirchen, Ober Ammergau, which disappointed me and little damaged Innsbruck, set in a valley with mountains towering above the town.

Berchtesgaden is a small village nestling at the foot of the mountains and high above you can see Hitler's eagle's nest perched precariously on a crag. You climb thousands of feet up an excellent road to Ober Salzburg, where eight or ten ruined buildings greet your eyes, the remains of Hitler's retreat. Here Hitler, Goring, Bormann, the architect had houses as well as SS barracks, a hotel, greenhouses all of which have been destroyed either by bombing, the SS or looted by successive visitors. Hitler's house must have been lovely. There is an enormous sitting room with a window like our mess in Algiers but twice as big, looking out over the mountains. At the other end an enormous fireplace – but everything has gone even the floorboards and over everything people have written their names. Behind Hitler's house there are about 100 steps leading down into the air raid shelter, a long passage out of which are rooms fitted with everything you could want, dentist, operating theatre, cinema, bedrooms, kitchen, bathrooms, wine cellar. Here there was no bomb damage, but the SS had had time to destroy or take away a good deal so have the Americans. I brought away a liquor glass!

About 20 minutes climb by car above that – it must be about 6.000ft up one comes to the eagle's nest itself, entered by a passage wide enough for a car about 100 yards into the mountain with a lift in the solid rock to the top. Here at last is the place from which Chamberlain brought back 'peace in our time', a largish villa, untouched by bombing and protected against looting, with an enormous conference room with a long table and about 30 chairs, a circular lounge with huge windows all round, kitchen and bedrooms etc, though the doors are all locked. Looking down from the balcony over Germany, Austria and Czechoslavakia it is so exhilarating that one feels – no! One is – omnipotent. And if one owned all that as Hitler did, how would one feel? God.

We came down to Konigsee, the petrol blue lake one could see like a mirror from the top – 200 feet deep, two miles wide and nearly five long, with the highest waterfall in Germany roaring down at one end and mountains towering up on every side.

From Salzburg we went down through beautiful little untouched Austria to Klagenfurt and the heart of Europe, where we sat and looked at the mountains of Yugoslavia ahead (Tito's bands come down on raiding parties into Austria) and the Hungarian mountains on the left.

On the way back from Klagenfurt to Salzburg we climbed up over Gross Glockner, 8,000ft high. We were in the clouds when we reached the top, and as it began to thunder and hail the mist lifted and we looked down on to the glacier 20 feet below us. It is about two miles long and a mile wide of solid ice, pitted and scored with pale translucent blue crevasses sloping up behind to the snow covered peak from which it originates. And as we picked edelweiss from the bank it started to get dark, and surely nothing could have been more lovely than this dim rain soaked evening on top of the world. Up there in the silence and wild magnificence (and soaked too to the skin) one felt more contented and peaceful than ever before.

The rest of the trip is comparatively of little interest – to Linz guarded on one side of the Danube by the Americans, on the other by the Russians, where we looked through a list of 150,000 names from one camp, to Chiemsee, a wild Scottish looking lake, where mad Ludwig built an imitation Versailles on an island, though we hadn't time to see it, and where finally he drowned himself and his doctor – back to Landshut where we sat at dusk on a huntsman's platform in the forest and tried to shoot deer, but none came and I was glad – through country where the rain had turned the mountain streams into roaring torrents, to commercial Germany once more and home.

There's so much more really, little pictures keep coming to my mind, like the evening near Regensburg when trying to find petrol we drove into a bombed out aerodrome and all you could see as the headlights picked them out, were bombed buildings, bomb craters and twisted hangers in an eerie desolate silence like the end of the world, and then the car ran out of petrol and there was no sound to break the stillness and one longed to run out of it screaming, only we were lost and didn't even know which way to run.

Or the night we were so behind schedule that we decided to go on driving and not stop, when we had three punctures between 6pm and 7.30am – and all the countless incredible places we slept in from a suite each in a first class hotel to a room shared with an American girl whilst Angus slept in the car, or one night when they tried to put the two of us in one room which had no window and nowhere to wash! –or the countless lunches we cooked ourselves over an open fire in the woods – or the masses and masses of ammunition, rifles, grenades and detonators left by the Germans lying in woods, by the side of roads, in streams where children can and do find them and blow themselves up – or the lines of little wooden crosses by the sides of roads which mark the graves of concentration camp victims now properly buried, but you'll be weary of reading if I go on any longer.

Love V.

My dear Vera,

[Censored] came back about two days ago, bringing with him [censored]. Apparently our new link, such as it is, couldn't be bothered to forward it, so I intend to send this to your home.

I'm sorry to hear you had such a dreary VE [Victory in Europe Day] – we did too, not that it was particularly dreary but simply that we never celebrated it as all as we were somewhere in the American zone, never really heard of it until afterwards!

I'm so glad you've at last got some leave, and I'm longing to hear how you got on with [censored], at least I think I am. I sit back as rather an old lady smiling benignly on the children, who think they're having a whale of a time and being such devils, when all the time I feel – we could teach them a thing or two – It's probably just as well really that they're not really so gay, the atmosphere is all wrong anyway, and they'd soon get every bad name – but it makes me feel very old. I wish you were here to gossip with.

Thank you for your efforts on behalf of Ruth Copp, it's all come through, but I felt very embarrassed as when I came back from seeing Judith Cotton and the other FANYs in Klagenfurt ... who all knew about it, I told her only to find she'd not heard about herself, so I had to do it circumspectly in case they'd got the name wrong.

I'm stricken with horror at the moment as here's a great rumour that Gamwell [Commandant of the FANY] is coming out here. We've heard so, and there are some other FANYs here, belonging to another lot who apparently know all about it. I'm rather worried since I haven't written to her since I've been out here and feel she's probably livid and therefore not telling us, and now of course it's much too obvious if I do write to her. I anticipate a terrific rocket!

Shall be only too pleased to look after Norman's brother if he comes out here. Why is his heart broken, have you failed in your matrimonial plans this time?

All the old familiar faces seem to be about here. I had dinner with Peter Stows one night and Tony Moore another, both of whom are working spitting distance of here.

I told you I wrote to Alastair before I left I think, but I've had no word so imagine I've had one. I was staggered at dinner the other night, because a girl here whom I know used to work for him suddenly said that all men with black hair and bright blue eyes are mad, she proceeded to give a perfect word picture of a man for whom she used to work and whom she didn't marry because he was mad – which was Alastair!! I think she must have forgotten that I knew she used to work for him, and that I couldn't fail to recognise the description – thus do we give ourselves away without mentioning names.

I'm so glad our trip to India is still on, I was so afraid that it might have been cancelled and that would be too awful. Do give my love to any old chums, and do try and come here when you come back, though where I shall be by then I'm not quite sure, the whole thing is so uncertain, though I think we might get in another trip or two maybe.

I'm glad that Fran is at last married, though I do share your views about it, it seems such a toss up. Perhaps all the FANYs in Poland will be able to spend their time visiting each other, though the best solution obviously is a kind of cosmopolitan life, outside the country of origin of both. Easier said than done.

Robin Brook expressed a wish to lunch with the FANYs of ME.42. I rang up today at 12.55 to ask if he could come in half an hour. I ask you, however in the usual style he was made to take pot luck. Perhaps I don't know him well enough or something, but he seemed awfully heavy weather, and a little too much on the side of the enemy with whom we appear to be going to be faced at any minute. Any news out there?

Can't think of any other news at the moment. I had quite a pleasant time while Angus was away doing very little work and playing tennis and swimming. Pleasant now but I don't much like the thought of the winter.

My love to you

V.

Fan recalls her career with the FANY

In 1944 Fan was asked by Maria Gamwell, Commandant of the First Aid Nursing Yeomanry, for a brief account of her service in the FANY/SOE.

My Dear Gamwell,

You have asked for a short letter on my FANY activities during the last three years. May I commence by thanking the FANY Corps for giving me the opportunity of three years so packed with interest that when I consider putting them on paper I feel a 'short letter' may be a misnomer.

It is difficult to explain the mixed emotions with which I was introduced to my new job, the thrill to learn that such activities as those controlled by SOE were actually taking place, and that I as a driver, was to take the smallest part. I am full of admiration for those men and women who were prepared to leave the friendly atmosphere created by their accompanying officer and RAF crew to jump out of an aeroplane, and descend into a country occupied by the enemy, taking a chance that they might not land where those arranged to meet them had been instructed to wait, or that the lights signalling a welcome below were perhaps operated by the Gestapo waiting to carry out unthinkable horrors to anyone who had the courage to return to his own country to work for the Resistance; the courage of these people when night after night they were keyed up to leave, and the weather would be persistently bad, or mechanical defects would prevent the aircraft from taking off.

Six months passed driving people who had stories to tell of incredible escapes and adventures, stories of amazing courage and self control, and then I was told to work in the office as well as drive. So I spent another six months in the Operation Section (at SOE/HQ 64 Baker Street), which meant that I not only drove to the airport and saw these people leave for their courageous tasks, but worked out the pin point on the map where they were to land.

FANYs had as the operative word in those days, 'cope'. My next job was to strain this word for me to its utmost. I joined the Naval Section. I went to Cornwall to do the secretarial work, run the mess, do the accounts, and be general factotum. This proved to be a most difficult passage as I was the only FANY and the domestic staff consisted of four WRENS, the cook being a Petty Officer which called for every ounce of tact I could produce as a Lance Corporal FANY in charge. We weathered this period until the day came when the Commander of the Station left to go overseas, a memorable day, dawning with the accompanying beautiful colouring of a Cornish autumn morning, and the two small French fishing vessels looking very trim with their new coats of paint sliding down the creek to face a journey of more than a thousand miles in November weather with the Mediterranean uncomfortably populated by the enemy.

Soon after this I received a letter asking me to go overseas and so in April 1943 I went to Algiers which was a great event for me as I had not been abroad before. During the 15 months I spent in Algiers my good fortune in meeting interesting people continued as I was by then working in the Liaison Section through which officers coming out of the field had to pass when reporting to Allied Forces HQ. One of the most interesting evenings was when I was invited by one of these officers to an informal dinner party being given by General Veleht, and had the good fortune to sit next to the General . (who incidentally spoke very good English), at dinner. His enthusiasm, patriotism, and devotion to Marshal Tito, and to

Yugoslavia, which was shown in his replies to my endless questions, were an inspiration. His delight was almost childlike on finding a book in the house of the Canadian Minister which we were visiting after dinner, which contained several prints of scenes in Yugoslavia, which allowed him to show me the beauties of the Dalmation coast.

During this time we were fortunate in living in what must have been the ideal camp, a group of villas set in a pine wood on the sea shore. We had Betty Sale as our senior FANY Officer and she did everything possible to care for the wellbeing of the girls. Great efforts were made in the way of self entertainment in the camp, and a theatre was built and seasonal shows produced by the staff. The final show was given at Whitsuntide 1943, and six of the FANYs from mess no.1 were inveigled into doing the 'Can Can'. I was included in this and made my positively first and last appearance. We had black stockings from the WRENS, dresses from the local (Algiers) Opera Company and all the other accessories by beg, borrow or steal. The rehearsals were taken very seriously under the guidance of Jackie Porter, but the first performance almost ended in disaster when the officers, mainly the senior ones, started barracking and reduced the already very shaky performers to a state of uncontrollable laughter. In fact it became difficult to define who was doing the entertaining.

In July the section, which consisted of Colonel (Dodds-Parker), Leonora Railton and myself moved to Naples, where we had an office in a villa overlooking the famous view of the Bay, and Vesuvius. This was another hectic spell as apart from the usual office work we had to do our own ciphering, and I had to run the house, armed with a dictionary as the domestic staff were all Italian. Owing to the fact that the villa was in Naples, and on the route to most places, the villa developed into a miniature transit camp, which added to the complications of administration and each day passed in a whirl of ciphering, (a new venture for me), the office work, and the worries of not enough beds, insufficient rations, or no transport to go to the airport to fetch people. I counted at least ten white hairs acquired during this period, but in spite of these problems, my good fortune in meeting interesting people held good, for many of the officers from the field who were going home, or had to report to AFHQ, came to stay at the villa en route. We heard stories of Rumania, Yugoslavia, Albania, Greece etc, some tragic, some amusing, but all intensely interesting, and all of them filled me with great admiration for those officers who go off, often into parts unknown to them, to live with the Partisans, to be constantly hounded by the Germans, and to face up to the constant fear that the supplies they have asked for may not reach them for some considerable time.

This phase of my FANY career came to an end at the end of September '43 when the Colonel (Dodds- Parker) returned to England and our office was transferred to AFHQ, and the staff trebled. I then had the opportunity of going to Rome (the Mecca for all FANYs on leave) for three days leave. Unfortunately on arrival there my sole ambition was to make up for my lack of sleep for three months so from a sightseeing point of view my leave was rather wasted. On my return from leave I handed over my housekeeping problems and took up my new job as ADC to the General (Stawell), with a considerable amount of trepidation as I could not quite see how my previous jobs as driver, housekeeper, mess secretary, administration, cipher clerk, would fit together as training for an ADC. However the fact that had had to adapt myself so many times already had been useful, for I found that an ADC is a general factotum.

In my first week I accompanied the General on a trip to Cairo, and then Athens. I had never been to either place before. The whole trip was extremely interesting both from the point of view of work, and the opportunities for sightseeing, visiting the Sphinx, the Pyramids, and the Temples. In Cairo we had a particularly entertaining lunch with an Hungarian VIP and his wife who had been recently brought out of Greece. Although they were rather careworn owing to their trials, they were thoroughly amusing, particularly when describing how the Partisans managed to produce a bath for the lady at intervals during their walk over the mountains. On another occasion we had lunch with a Greek Resistance leader who had put up a grand performance during the occupation.

From Cairo we flew to Athens arriving six days after the German withdrawal, when the sight of a British uniform was still a novelty greeted with great enthusiasm – a fact I had forgotten when coming direct from the airport to the hotel by car I went straight up to my room to be 'attacked' by two chambermaids who were making the bed. They insisted on patting and kissing me to such an embarrassing extent that I fled downstairs and had lunch unwashed. The next morning I decided to explore the town whilst the General was at a meeting, and shaken hands several times with Greeks who wished to express their welcome, I was followed by a man with a camera and as my bright smile (as I thought) was by now developing into a set grimace, this was too much and I fled for the hotel. But in that short walk, and the outings I subsequently had with the General, you could feel the warmth of the welcome and the sense of relief which hung over the town at long last freed from their oppressors.

A dinner party was given by our office during the General's stay in honour of the arrival of a Greek General, who, with his band of resistance fighters, had been a constant thorn in the flesh of the Germans during their occupation. Having been to Athens and felt the sense of relief and welcome to the British, the present [1944] news of the necessity for British troops to fire on Greek people is doubly tragic.

At the time of writing working for the General has been full of interest, and I consider myself extremely fortunate in having the opportunity to see such places as Rome, Sienna and other notable places in Italy which have been included in the General's tours. These visits have invariably included the opportunity to meet officers who had returned from Partisan lands, and actual leaders of the resistance. A particularly interesting time was when the Delegates of the Liberation Committee for Northern Italy came to the South to endeavour with our organisation to draw up an agreement between Senior Allied Command, the Italian Government and themselves. On first meeting the head of the delegation I immediately thought of the type of person who is Manager of your local bank, a quiet, paternal, rather plump man of about 50 years. When talking to him I realised that this impression was quite incorrect. The quiet paternal air was merely the cover for the long patience he had learnt in the face of adversity in his endeavour to keep alive resistance, and to save Italy from Fascism and the Germans.

Yours Sincerely

Captain Vera Aungiers FANY/SOE.

The End of the War

These documents and letters recall the end of Fan's war career. Notice her new name: she has married Lieutenant-Colonel Hewlett. Women's Transport Service (FANY),

55/56 Sloane Street, London, SW1
19 Dec 46

GENERAL ORDER NO. 2/46 FROM THE COMMANDING OFFICER AND REGIMENTAL BOARD TO ALL MEMBERS OF THE WTS/FANY CORPS

Subject: RANK

At their meetings on 28th October 1946 and 6th December 1946, the Commanding Officer and Regimental Board decided that the moratorium on war ranks held throughout the WTS/FANY should end on 31st December 1946.

In order to make a practical proposition of the re-organisation of the Corps on to a peace-time basis, (and in accordance with Corps precedents after the last war,) all members of the Corps will revert to the status of ordinary members, with the exception of the

Regimental Board who, (for continuity of administration) must retain their Officer-status while holding their appointments as members of the Regimental Board in accordance with the Constitution and Standing Orders of the Corps. (See standing orders Para. 2, sub paras 1, 5, 9, and 11.)

Members of the Regimental Board who do not hold any other specific Corps appointment on Headquarters Staff, Staff Officers to HRH the Commandant-in-Chief, or appointments to Group, Company or Section Officer rank made since June 1946, will carry the rank of Captain. Membership of the Board remains a Staff appointment. See Standing Orders para 2, sub para 10.)

Appointments to Headquarters Staff, Group, Company and Section Establishments will be made as required by the Commanding Officer and Regimental Board, and the rank of any such appointment will be held during their term of service in that appointment.

FANY members *still serving overseas* with AWS or holding specific appointments with Control Commissions, or other Military or Government services, *will retain their war rank* and be available for promotion as required *until demobilisation plus 28 days,* after which they will revert to ordinary membership.

WTS/FANY members still serving in the official women's services (WRNS, ATS and WAAF) will continue to hold honorary FANY rank equivalent to their service ranks until demobilised. When demobilised, reversion, with eligibility to some new appointment in the Corps as required, will take place in the same way as for Corps members.

The Commanding Officer and Regimental Board will survey the requirements of the Corps for officers and NCOs to fill peace-time Headquarters, Group, Company and Section establishments. No peacetime appointments will be made unless members are assisting with the work, administration of, and training in, the peace-time organisation; and a due and proper sense of responsibility in such work will be required; but, in the making of appointments, suitability and war service will be carefully considered.

All members of the Corps, whether ex-officers, war-time members, or new members, will henceforward be eligible for recommendation to fill vacancies on establishments, according to the Constitution and Standing Orders of the Corps (and subject to their ability to pass such tests and examinations as may be laid down from time to time by the Commanding Officer and Regimental Board), by selection on qualifications and personal qualities and availability, from lists submitted as required to the Commanding Officer, by the Group and Company Commanders. All recommendations for appointments must be made through Company and Group channels.

NOTE: FANY REGIMENTAL CLUB

It is pointed out to all FANYs that membership of the Club or election to any of the Club Committees does not in itself carry any Regimental rank, nor do the Club Committees or Club Staff appointments count as any part of the Corps establishment.

Commanding Officer, FANY Corps.

Room 98
The Horse Guards,
Whitehall, SW1
From: The Finance Officer (FANY)
STS HQ
AVH/FOP/343
21th September 1945

Mrs. J. Hewlett,
Greenbank,
Eldwick Road,
West Hartlepool,
Durham.

PAY AND ALLOWANCES

(1)   Pay Slip is attached, from which you will observe that Pay and Allowances to the date of your out-posting, i.e., 27/10/45 are being transferred to your Banking Account.

(2)   National Health and Unemployment Insurance Cards are also enclosed and I shall be obliged if you will sign and return the attached form of receipt.

(3)   Income Tax Form P.45 is attached, which should be disposed of in accordance with the instructions thereon. In this connection P.50 is

enclosed, which will enable you to claim a refund of Income Tax in due course.

Lieut/FANY
For Finance Officer

Form F/9
From: The Finance Officer, STS HQ
To Capt. V.M. Aungiers

£. S. D.

Income Tax   11.13 .00
Pay   23.11.06
                    20.18.06
N.H.I.   12.08   Allowances14.8
1.6.1   5.2.6
Cash paid to your Bankers   50.17.9
On 26.9.45   £66.9.6
                                 £64.9.6

Major
Finance Officer

Now married and in Hartlepool, Fan subscribes to the Special Services Club, and is thanked by the Commandant

The winding up of SOE.
As from
31a Wilton Place,
London, SW1
March 12th 1946

Dear Hewlett,
Your letter and cheque arrived just as I was leaving the office this evening and I brought it home to answer. You must forgive a typewritten letter, but I find it much easier to write at some length on the typewriter, and I dare say you would like to have what news there is.

Thank you so much for your subscription and very kind donation to the club. It is indeed good of you to send us this as I know what a business it must be setting up house yourself. It is most welcome. This is quite the worst time to embark on a venture of this nature; everything is very expensive and the restrictions have to be encountered to be believed! However, we are progressing slowly. And it was a case of going ahead now or not at all. I hope the club will prove to be a happy meeting ground for all FANYs in the future. We are very lucky to have been able to get accommodation in such a central neighbourhood, and the FANYs will have two houses which really belong to them for twenty-two years. At the end of that time I hope they will be very flourishing and able to find something equally suitable to fill their needs.

I so much appreciated your very kind congratulations on my award. It was really given in recognition of the splendid work all the FANYs have done during the war. It isn't a personal award. I am very proud to have been one of you.

As far as you yourself are concerned, I feel sure you must be proud of your contribution to the work of SOE and through them, to the whole war effort. It was simply splendid, and I hope has given you some happy memories.

I wonder if you have heard that Betty Sale has married Major Rigg out in Hobart, Tasmania. They are coming home and should be on the way now, and they are going to settle permanently in Sheffield. I haven't got their address here, but if you want it at any time FANY HQ will always have it, or would forward a letter.

S.O.E is practically liquidated now. In fact the FANY office, Finance, Security and one or two other small branches are all that is left. The Indian FANY section are returning fast now and we hope will all be back by the end of April.

As you know Hope had been suffering from acute attacks of pain in her back for about eighteen months, so she decided, on the recommendation of her doctor, to return to our home in N. Rhodesia. She left by air on December 20th and arrived home on the 29th. Since then she has had a bad attack of 'flu', but she says she has quite forgotten about her back now she is out in the sunshine and a warm climate. I don't expect to be able to join her until the end of the autumn.

Margaret Jackson has found her way out to Austria. I have not heard more than that.

We are busy demobilising and getting FANYs into jobs they like. They are being offered very good jobs, both at home and abroad. We are having lots of good contacts and employers seem willing to pay higher salaries to FANYs than to anyone else.

You will be interested and possibly amused to hear that the FANY Corps Units are to be represented in the Army Section of the Victory March. We are to form the rear contingent of this section. The allotment of representation is one row for every ten thousand in each particular arm, of the service. Strictly speaking we should only have at most one row, however, we have been allotted two and an officer is to lead, and there is to be a FANY canteen in the MT column. After having spent such an indeterminate existence during the war, neither fish, flesh fowl, but presumably good red herring, we end up with the Army!

I am afraid the broadcast has got bogged down, at any rate for the time being. In the end, the General [Colin Gubbins, CO of the SOE] felt he couldn't do it, and by the time security had relaxed sufficiently to allow us to put across a really interesting talk, the BBC wasn't interested. We have tried to get some publicity in the papers, but they too say the public doesn't want any more war news. It is very disappointing, but perhaps if we prepare sufficiently long beforehand we might do something round about June 8th when every-one will be thinking more about the services. The truth of the matter is that UNO and all the chaotic happenings all over the world have provided all the material the papers are able to print with the very small allotment of paper they are allowed.

I did a broadcast on the African Service in 1942, and Hope found when she got out there again that East Africa knew much more about the FANYs than anyone knows in this country, and were much more interested in us.

With all good wishes, and thank you again so much for your most welcome donation to the Club.

Yours very sincerely

Marian Gamwell

Fan's son is born

9a Kensington Court Mews, W8
18th July 1947.

My dearest V,
We were so happy to hear of Nicholas; safe arrival and offer you our very warm congratulations; I hope he will like his nursery – did you manage to find all the little items you wanted? Do let me know if there is anything you would like from London as I have much more free time now that I have given up the Wimpole St. Job.

We haven't heard when we shall be leaving the UK and expect to have the usual rush as these Govt types take so long with all the papers! In the meantime, John is on a refresher course of midwifery and trots off to Lewisham hospital every afternoon. You mention that the venture will really be pioneering – I hope to god that it won't be!!?? Actually, it is a very civilised island but like everywhere else, we may have a job to find a house or bungalow to our liking and have to take 'what's going'. We have met a doctor and his wife who have spent 8 years out there and they are going back to retire as they like it so much – they were able to give us lots of useful information.

Yes, Mary McV. is married to her Roger and is living in Paris but we haven't had any news from her since she was here at Easter.

Betty Sale was quite cheerful when I saw her and of course, I didn't mention the word marriage or of anything connected with it but she did say of her own accord that she was busy trying to straighten out her private affairs but I didn't enlarge on the subject. I saw Valery last week in the Club and also Sheila Riesco who seems to be very happily married. Leo was also there and Barbara Tims and Gerry Holdsworth put in an appearance – said that he was not doing much work and found time for drinking but he need not have mentioned it as his looks rather betrayed him!!! Oh! Gundrid was also there one night, very chatty and friendly, she has returned from Trieste so as to look after her father who is ill.

We went to see Yvonne Arnaud in 'Jane' a week or so ago and thoroughly agree with your opinion of it – quite one of the best plays now running. We pop down to Rankins most week-ends to enjoy some fresh air and fishing but my brother is coming up tonight and tomorrow we are going to see 'Birds eye view' which I hear is very amusing.

Discovered some days ago that Anthony Butler lives practically opposite us in Edmond Court – but as yet, haven't met him!! I saw Dodds-Parker, now an MP, when we were in the House of Commons two weeks ago – listening to the Electricity Bill being passed, but didn't have the opportunity of speaking to him.

Will certainly let you know when we hear any more news of our departure.

Lots of Love to you both

Always

Joan.

'The Tin Gee Gee'

I'm sure Fan sees a moral in this children's poem, but I think I will let you, dear reader, work out for yourself what it might be!

'The Tin Gee Gee'

I was strolling one day down the Lowther arcade
That place for children's toys
Where you may purchase a dolly or a spade
For your good little girls and boys
And as I passed a certain stall
Said a little tin voice to me
Oh! I am a soldier in a little cocked hat
And I ride on a tin gee gee
Oh! I am a soldier in a little cocked hat
And I ride on a tin gee gee.
So I looked, and little tin soldier I saw
In his little cocked hat so fine
He'd a little tin sword that shone in the light
As he led the glittering line
Of tin Huzzas whose sabres flashed
In a manner a la milataree
And the little tin soldier he rode at the head

So proud on his tin gee gee
And the little tin soldier he rode at the head
So proud on his tin gee gee.
Now the little tin soldier he bobbed and he sighed
So I patted his little tin head
'What vexes your little tin head' I said?
And this is what he said
'I've been on this stall a very long time
And I'm marked 1 shilling 9 pence you see
While just on the shelf above my head
There's a fellow marked 2/3
Now he hasn't got a horse and he hasn't got a sword
And I'm twice as good as he
So why mark me at 1/9
And him at 2/3?'
There's a saucy little dolly girl over there
And I'm madly in love with she
But now that I'm only marked 1/9
She turns up her nose at me
She turns up her little wax nose at me
And carries on with 2/3
And oh she's dressed in a beautiful dress
It's a dress I do admire
She has pearly blue eyes that open and shut
When worked inside by a wire
And once on a time when folks were gone
She used to flirt with me
But now that I'm only marked 1/9 she turns up her nose at me
She turns up her little wax nose at me
And carries on with 2/3.'
'Cheer up my little tin man' said I
'I'll see what I can do
You're a fine little fellow and it is a shame
That she should so treat you'

9 780957 305878